CAMBRIDGE

AMERICAN EMPOWER

STUDENT'S BOOK B
WITH DIGITAL PACK

T0349641

C1
ADVANCED

Adrian Doff, Craig Thaine
Herbert Puchta, Jeff Stranks, Peter Lewis-Jones
with Mark Hancock and Wayne Rimmer

CAMBRIDGE

AMERICAN EMPOWER is a six-level general English course for adult and young adult learners, taking students from beginner to advanced level (CEFR A1 to C1). *American Empower* combines course content from Cambridge University Press with validated assessment from the experts at Cambridge Assessment English.

American Empower's unique mix of engaging classroom materials and reliable assessment enables learners to make consistent and measurable progress.

Content you'll love.

Assessment you

can trust.

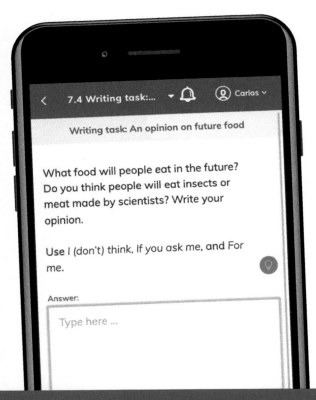

Better Learning with *American Empower*

Better Learning is our simple approach where **insights** we've gained from research have helped shape **content** that drives **results**.

Learner engagement

1 Content that informs and motivates

Insights
Sustained motivation is key to successful language learning and skills development.

Content
Clear learning goals, thought-provoking images, texts, and speaking activities, plus video content to arouse curiosity.

Results
Content that surprises, entertains, and provokes an emotional response, helping teachers to deliver motivating and memorable lessons.

6A WE ALL SEEM TO LOVE TAKING PICTURES

Learn to describe photos and hobbies
- Simple and continuous verbs
- Adjectives: describing images

1 SPEAKING AND READING

a Answer the questions.
1 What do you usually use to take photos – your phone or a camera?
2 Do you take a lot of photos? Why / Why not?
3 What do you usually do with the photos?
4 Do you think you're good at taking photos? Why / Why not?

b Have you ever heard of the photographer Elliott Erwitt? Read the fact file on p. 69. What kind of photographs does he take?

c What do you think are important skills for photographers? Think about these things:
- what you choose to photograph
- the way the photos look
- the equipment you use
- your attitude and personality.

d Read the article. Are any of your ideas from 1c mentioned?

e Read the article again. Answer the questions.
1 Why shouldn't street photographers plan much?
2 What should be the aim of a street photograph, according to Elliott Erwitt and the writer?
3 What do you think Elliott Erwitt means by *visual garbage*?
4 What attributes does the writer think are most important in a street photographer?
5 What does the writer mean when he talks about keeping an alien mindset?

f Answer the questions.
1 How are Erwitt's methods and style evident in the photo of the Villa Borghese Gardens? What do you think of the photograph?
2 Answer the question at the end of the article: As an alien – what would you find intriguing, amusing, or nonsensical?
3 Look at the titles of the "lessons" (1–4) in the article. Are they relevant to other skills and/or jobs that you know about?

2 VOCABULARY Adjectives: describing images

a Work with a partner. What do the highlighted adjectives in the article mean? Check your ideas in a dictionary.

b Now go to Vocabulary Focus 6A on p. 163.

Villa Borghese Gardens, Rome 1969 by Elliott Erwitt

UNIT 6

ELLIOTT ERWITT PHOTOGRAPHER FACT FILE
- born in Paris, brought up in Italy, moved to the U.S. at age 10
- began photography career in the 1950s
- known for advertising and street photography, particularly ironic black-and-white shots of everyday life
- invited to join the internationally famous photography agency Magnum in 1953

Lessons Elliott Erwitt Has Taught Me about STREET PHOTOGRAPHY by Eric Kim

If you are not familiar with the work of Elliott Erwitt, you may perhaps have seen some of his iconic work from around the globe (the picture opposite was taken by him). He had one of the longest careers of any photographer, spanning over 50 years.
What I most appreciate about Elliott Erwitt is his wry sense of humor when looking at the world – as well as his straightforward philosophies about photography. In this article, I share some of his thoughts and advice.

1 DON'T PLAN TOO MUCH – WANDER AROUND
I think that as a street photographer, sometimes I fall into a trap of planning too much. I generally try to focus my attention on projects (having a preconceived project in mind when shooting in the streets), but I often find it also takes away from the shooting experience. One of the best things about street photography is to be a flaneur – someone who wanders around without a specific destination in mind.
ERWITT *I don't start out with any specific interests; I just react to what I see.*
Takeaway point: Let your curiosity lead you. Just go out and shoot whatever you find interesting. Go down roads that may seem a little foreign, and you might be lucky enough to stumble upon great street photography shots.

2 FOCUS ON CONTENT OVER FORM
Great photos are a combination of content (what is happening in the frame) as well as form (composition). But which is more important? Content or form?
ERWITT *My wish for the future of photography is that it might continue to have some relevance to the human condition and might represent work that evokes knowledge and emotions. That photography has content rather than just form. And I hope that there will be enough produce to balance out the visual garbage that one sees in our current life.*
Takeaway point: We often find fascinating characters in the street and take photos of them, but the compositions may not be so good. On the other hand, we might take well-composed photos of a street scene, but there is nothing going on in the photo – it is boring and without soul.
I agree with Erwitt that we should, as street photographers, put more emphasis on content over form. I feel that photos that evoke emotions and the human condition are far more powerful and meaningful than just photos with good composition.

3 DON'T TAKE THINGS TOO SERIOUSLY
When one thinks about the photography agency Magnum, some adjectives that come to mind are gritty and raw.
However, Erwitt's style was vastly different. He didn't go out and take photos in conflicts or war. His photos tended to be more playful, humorous, and amusing.
ERWITT *Well, I'm not a serious photographer like most of my colleagues. That is to say, I'm serious about not being serious.*
Takeaway point: Don't take yourself and your street photography too seriously, and remember – at the end of the day you want to enjoy yourself.

4 HONE YOUR SKILLS OF OBSERVATION
Erwitt was inspired to go out and take pictures when he saw a photograph by master photographer Henri Cartier-Bresson. He realized it was an act of observation that made the photo great and that he could do something similar.
ERWITT *The picture seemed evocative and emotional. Also, a simple observation was all that it took to produce it. I thought, if one could make a living out of doing such pictures that would be desirable.*
Takeaway point: One of the things that is the most beautiful about street photography is that it doesn't rely on having an expensive camera or exotic lenses. Rather, it comes down to having an observant and curious eye for people and the world around you.
Therefore, cultivate your vision and way of seeing the world. I recommend that you always carry a camera with you because you never know when the best street photo opportunities will present themselves to you.
A fun exercise: Pretend that you are an alien from another planet, and you have come to the planet Earth for the first time. Imagine how strange human beings would seem – and the urban environment they have built for themselves. As an alien, what would you find intriguing, amusing, or nonsensical? Always keep that mindset to be amazed by what you see around you.

68

69

---

2 Personalized and relevant

Insights
Language learners benefit from frequent opportunities to personalize their responses.

Content
Personalization tasks in every unit make the target language more meaningful to the individual learner.

Results
Personal responses make learning more memorable and inclusive, with all students participating in spontaneous spoken interaction.

> "There are so many adjectives to describe such a wonderful series, but in my opinion it's very reliable, practical, and modern."
>
> **Zenaide Brianez, Director of Studies, Instituto da Língua Inglesa, Brazil**

Measurable progress

1 Assessment you can trust

Insights
Tests developed and validated by Cambridge Assessment English, the world leaders in language assessment, to ensure they are accurate and meaningful.

Content
End-of-unit tests, mid- and end-of-course competency tests, and personalized CEFR test report forms provide reliable information on progress with language skills.

Results
Teachers can see learners' progress at a glance, and learners can see measurable progress, which leads to greater motivation.

Results of an impact study showing % improvement of Reading levels, based on global *Empower* students' scores over one year.

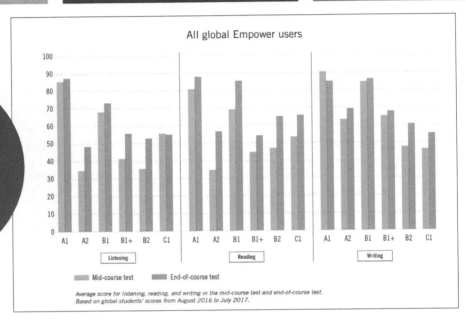

Average score for listening, reading, and writing in the mid-course test and end-of-course test.
Based on global students' scores from August 2016 to July 2017.

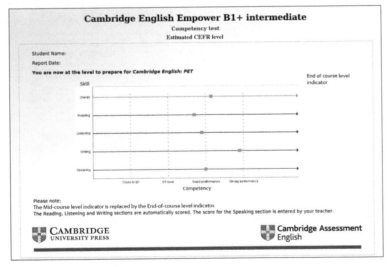

> **We started using the tests provided with Empower and our students started showing better results from this point until now.**
>
> Kristina Ivanova, Director of Foreign Language Training Centre, ITMO University, Saint Petersburg, Russia

2 Evidence of impact

Insights
Schools and colleges need to show that they are evaluating the effectiveness of their language programs.

Content
Empower (British English) impact studies have been carried out in various countries, including Russia, Brazil, Turkey, and the UK, to provide evidence of positive impact and progress.

Results
Colleges and universities have demonstrated a significant improvement in language level between the mid- and end-of-course tests, as well as a high level of teacher satisfaction with *Empower*.

Manageable learning

1 Mobile friendly

Insights
Learners expect online content to be mobile friendly but also flexible and easy to use on any digital device.

Content
American Empower provides easy access to Digital Workbook content that works on any device and includes practice activities with audio.

Results
Digital Workbook content is easy to access anywhere, and produces meaningful and actionable data so teachers can track their students' progress and adapt their lesson accordingly.

> " *I had been studying English for 10 years before university, and I didn't succeed. But now with Empower I know my level of English has changed.* "

Nikita, *Empower* Student, ITMO University, Saint Petersburg, Russia

2 Corpus-informed

Insights
Corpora can provide valuable information about the language items learners are able to learn successfully at each CEFR level.

Content
Two powerful resources – Cambridge Corpus and English Profile – informed the development of the *Empower* course syllabus and the writing of the materials.

Results
Learners are presented with the target language they are able to incorporate and use at the right point in their learning journey. They are not overwhelmed with unrealistic learning expectations.

Rich in practice

1 Language in use

Insights
It is essential that learners are offered frequent and manageable opportunities to practice the language they have been focusing on.

Content
Throughout the *American Empower* Student's Book, learners are offered a wide variety of practice activities, plenty of controlled practice, and frequent opportunities for communicative spoken practice.

Results
Meaningful practice makes new language more memorable and leads to more efficient progress in language acquisition.

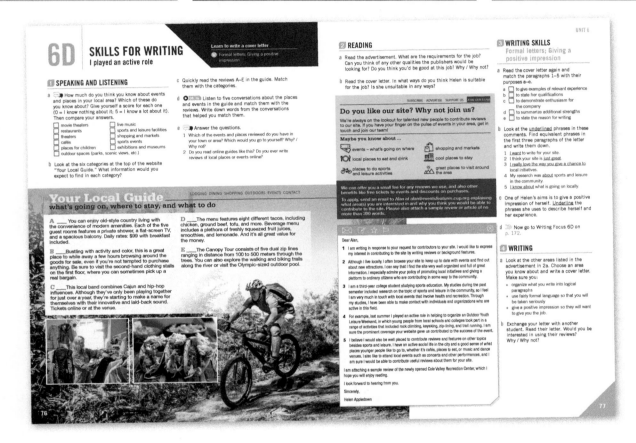

2 Beyond the classroom

There are plenty of opportunities for personalization.

**Elena Pro,
Teacher, EOI
de San Fernando
de Henares,
Spain**

Insights
Progress with language learning often requires work outside of the classroom, and different teaching models require different approaches.

Content
American Empower is available with a print workbook, online practice, documentary-style videos that expose learners to real-world English, plus additional resources with extra ideas and fun activities.

Results
This choice of additional resources helps teachers to find the most effective ways to motivate their students both inside and outside the classroom.

Unit overview

Unit Opener

Getting started page – Clear learning objectives to give an immediate sense of purpose.

Lessons A and B

Grammar and Vocabulary – Input and practice of core grammar and vocabulary, plus a mix of skills.

Digital Workbook (online, mobile): Grammar and Vocabulary

Lesson C

Everyday English – Functional language in common, everyday situations.

Digital Workbook (online, mobile): Listening and Speaking

Unit Progress Test

Lesson D

Integrated Skills – Practice of all four skills, with a special emphasis on writing.

Digital Workbook (online, mobile): Reading and Writing

Review

Extra practice of grammar, vocabulary, and pronunciation. Also a "Review your progress" section for students to reflect on the unit.

Mid- / End-of-course test

Additional practice

Further practice is available for outside of the class with these components.

Digital Workbook (online, mobile)

Workbook (printed)

Components

Resources – Available on cambridgeone.org

- Audio
- Video
- Unit Progress Tests (Print)
- Unit Progress Tests (Online)
- Mid- and end-of-course assessment (Print)
- Mid- and end-of-course assessment (Online)
- Digital Workbook (Online)
- Photocopiable Grammar, Vocabulary, and Pronunciation worksheets

This page is intentionally left blank.

✪ CAN DO OBJECTIVES

- Describe photos and hobbies
- Tell a descriptive narrative
- Organize a presentation
- Write a cover letter

PERSPECTIVES

UNIT 6

GETTING STARTED

a 💬 Look at the picture and answer the questions.
1 What are the people doing? Why do you think they're doing it?
2 How long do you think it has taken them? How long do you think it will stay?
3 What impact do you think it will have on passersby?

b 💬 Answer the questions.
1 Are there any examples of street art in your town or city?
2 How do you think your community would react to having a piece of street art like the one in the photo on their street?

6A | WE ALL SEEM TO LOVE TAKING PICTURES

Learn to describe photos and hobbies

G Simple and continuous verbs
V Adjectives: describing images

1 SPEAKING AND READING

a 💬 Answer the questions.

1 What do you usually use to take photos – your phone or a camera?
2 Do you take a lot of photos? Why / Why not?
3 What do you usually do with the photos?
4 Do you think you're good at taking photos? Why / Why not?

b 💬 Have you ever heard of the photographer Elliott Erwitt? Read the fact file on p. 69. What kind of photographs does he take?

c 💬 What do you think are important skills for photographers? Think about these things:

- what you choose to photograph
- the way the photos look
- the equipment you use
- your attitude and personality.

d Read the article. Are any of your ideas from 1c mentioned?

e Read the article again. Answer the questions.

1 Why shouldn't street photographers plan much?
2 What should be the aim of a street photograph, according to Elliott Erwitt and the writer?
3 What do you think Elliott Erwitt means by *visual garbage*?
4 What attributes does the writer think are most important in a street photographer?
5 What does the writer mean when he talks about keeping an alien mindset?

f 💬 Answer the questions.

1 How are Erwitt's methods and style evident in the photo of the Villa Borghese Gardens? What do you think of the photograph?
2 Answer the question at the end of the article: As an alien – what would you find intriguing, amusing, or nonsensical?
3 Look at the titles of the "lessons" (1–4) in the article. Are they relevant to other skills and/or jobs that you know about?

2 VOCABULARY Adjectives: describing images

a 💬 Work with a partner. What do the highlighted adjectives in the article mean? Check your ideas in a dictionary.

b ≫ Now go to Vocabulary Focus 6A on p. 163.

Villa Borghese Gardens, Rome 1969 by Elliott Erwitt

ELLIOTT ERWITT: PHOTOGRAPHER FACT FILE

- born in Paris, brought up in Italy, moved to the U.S. at age 10
- began photography career in the 1950s
- known for advertising and street photography, particularly ironic black-and-white shots of everyday life
- invited to join the internationally famous photography agency Magnum in 1953

Lessons Elliott Erwitt Has Taught Me about STREET PHOTOGRAPHY

by Eric Kim

If you are not familiar with the work of Elliott Erwitt, you may perhaps have seen some of his iconic work from around the globe (the picture opposite was taken by him). He had one of the longest careers of any photographer, spanning over 50 years.

What I most appreciate about Elliott Erwitt is his wry sense of humor when looking at the world – as well as his straightforward philosophies about photography. In this article, I share some of his thoughts and advice.

1 DON'T PLAN TOO MUCH – WANDER AROUND

I think that as a street photographer, sometimes I fall into a trap of planning too much. I generally try to focus my attention on projects (having a preconceived project in mind when shooting in the streets), but I often find it also takes away from the shooting experience. One of the best things about street photography is to be a flaneur – someone who wanders around without a specific destination in mind.

ERWITT *I don't start out with any specific interests; I just react to what I see.*

Takeaway point: Let your curiosity lead you. Just go out and shoot whatever you find interesting. Go down roads that may seem a little foreign, and you might be lucky enough to stumble upon great street photography shots.

2 FOCUS ON CONTENT OVER FORM

Great photos are a combination of content (what is happening in the frame) as well as form (composition). But which is more important? Content or form?

ERWITT *My wish for the future of photography is that it might continue to have some relevance to the human condition and might represent work that evokes knowledge and emotions. That photography has content rather than just form. And I hope that there will be enough produce to balance out the visual garbage that one sees in our current life.*

Takeaway point: We often find fascinating characters in the street and take photos of them, but the compositions may not be so good. On the other hand, we might take well-composed photos of a street scene, but there is nothing going on in the photo – it is boring and without soul.

I agree with Erwitt that we should, as street photographers, put more emphasis on content over form. I feel that photos that evoke emotions and the human condition are far more powerful and meaningful than just photos with good composition.

3 DON'T TAKE THINGS TOO SERIOUSLY

When one thinks about the photography agency Magnum, some adjectives that come to mind are *gritty* and *raw*.

However, Erwitt's style was vastly different. He didn't go out and take photos in conflicts or war. His photos tended to be more playful, humorous, and amusing.

ERWITT *Well, I'm not a serious photographer like most of my colleagues. That is to say, I'm serious about not being serious.*

Takeaway point: Don't take yourself and your street photography too seriously, and remember – at the end of the day you want to enjoy yourself.

4 HONE YOUR SKILLS OF OBSERVATION

Erwitt was inspired to go out and take pictures when he saw a photograph by master photographer Henri Cartier-Bresson. He realized it was an act of observation that made the photo great and that he could do something similar.

ERWITT *The picture seemed evocative and emotional. Also, a simple observation was all that it took to produce it. I thought, if one could make a living out of doing such pictures that would be desirable.*

Takeaway point: One of the things that is the most beautiful about street photography is that it doesn't rely on having an expensive camera or exotic lenses. Rather, it comes down to having an observant and curious eye for people and the world around you.

Therefore, cultivate your vision and way of seeing the world. I recommend that you always carry a camera with you because you never know when the best street photo opportunities will present themselves to you.

A fun exercise: Pretend that you are an alien from another planet, and you have come to the planet Earth for the first time. Imagine how strange human beings would seem – and the urban environment they have built for themselves. As an alien, what would you find intriguing, amusing, or nonsensical?

Always keep that mindset to be amazed by what you see around you.

3 LISTENING

a 💬📱 Who do you know who is passionate about their hobby? What does the person's hobby involve?

b ▶06.03 Listen to Monika, an amateur photographer. Do you think Monika is passionate about photography? Why?

Monika, amateur photographer

A recent photo taken by Monika

c ▶06.03 Listen again and answer the questions.
1 What motivated Monika to learn more about photography? Why did she decide to take a course?
2 How has she improved since she started the course?
3 Why does Monika like the photo she took, on the right?
4 How does she describe her other favorite photograph?

d 💬📱 Do you think Monika would agree with Elliott Erwitt's lessons? Why / Why not?

4 GRAMMAR
Simple and continuous verbs

a ▶06.04 Which verb form in *italics* did you hear in the interview with Monika? Listen and check.

So, ¹*do you feel / are you feeling* more confident with your camera now?
It ²*depends / is depending* on the types of photo that I want to take.
Have you ³*discovered / been discovering* any bad habits since you ⁴*started / were starting* your class?
I ⁵*took / was taking* photos of everything, and I wasn't really following any rules.
When I ⁶*take / 'm taking* my photos now, I'm more cautious and kind of careful how I do it.
I ⁷*think / am thinking* I have two pictures that are my favorite pictures.
I chose this building that is supposed to be demolished. Actually, it ⁸*is demolished / is being demolished* now.

b Look at the verb forms in the sentences in 4a. Match each example 1–8 with one or more descriptions below.

The verb is … .
- simple for a verb not usually used in the continuous ☐
- simple for a completed action ☐ ☐
- simple for general truth or attitude ☐ ☐ ☐
- continuous to describe a repeated action ☐
- continuous to focus on the duration of an action ☐
- continuous for an action in progress at a particular time ☐
- a verb with different meanings in the simple and continuous. ☐

c Look at the verb forms 1, 5, and 6 in 4a again. In each case, is the alternative verb form possible? If so, would the meaning be different?

d ≫ Now go to Grammar Focus 6A on p. 148.

e In each sentence below, find a verb that would be better in the continuous and change it.
1 My little brother always asks me to play computer games with him, but I find them really boring.
2 By this time next month, I'll have played volleyball for three years.
3 These days everyone appears to use a tablet in class rather than writing in a notebook.
4 I often make mistakes when I'm not careful.
5 I've looked for a good grammar app, but I can't find one that's free.

f 💬📱 Change the sentences in 4e to make them true for you. Compare your ideas with a partner.

5 SPEAKING

a 💬📱 Answer the questions.
1 What is your favorite photo of yourself? Describe it to your partner. Say why you like it.
2 What's the best / funniest / most beautiful photo you've ever taken? What's the story behind the picture?

b 💬📱 What kind of visual art interests you most? Think about:
- painting
- interior design
- drawing
- sculpture
- cartoons
- fashion.

c 💬📱 Tell your partner about:
1 how you became interested
2 what specifically you like
3 where and how often you look at it
4 any ways you can learn more about this.

d 💬📱 Do you and your partner share any interests in this area?

6B A PERSON WAVING FOR HELP

1 VOCABULARY Emotions

a 💬 Which of the adjectives in the box have *positive* (P) or *negative* (N) meaning?

helpless	disillusioned
overjoyed	overexcited
satisfied	gleeful

b ▶ 06.07 Look at the adjectives in **bold**. Match the feelings 1–8 with their continuations a–h. Listen and check.

1. ☐ I was absolutely **devastated**.
2. ☐ I felt very **frustrated**.
3. ☐ I was terribly **restless**.
4. ☐ I felt extremely **jealous**.
5. ☐ I felt a bit **insecure**.
6. ☐ I was totally **speechless**.
7. ☐ I feel so **ashamed**.
8. ☐ I felt absolutely **petrified**.

a It was the most beautiful thing I'd ever seen.

b I needed to get in touch, but I couldn't track her down.

c My behavior at the party was unforgivable.

d It was the biggest game of the year, and we had played appallingly.

e I was the only person at the party who was over 40.

f My brother had money, friends, and now a charming wife.

g I couldn't concentrate on my book or TV or work.

h There was a snake crawling across my foot.

c 💬 Write sentences like 1b a–h for the emotions in 1a. Read them to other students. Can they guess the feeling?

d ▶ 06.08 **Pronunciation** Listen to these pairs of sentences from 1b and mark the main stress. How is the stress different in the a and the b sentences? Which show stronger feelings?

1. a I'm absolutely devastated.
   b I'm absolutely devastated.
2. a I felt extremely jealous.
   b I felt extremely jealous.
3. a I feel so ashamed.
   b I feel so ashamed.

e 💬 Take turns reading aloud your sentences from 1c showing strong feelings. Ask your partner questions to continue the conversation.

2 READING

a 💬 Read one of the two eyewitness accounts of the same incident. Student A: Read the blog "Brad's View." Student B: Read the email "Martha's View." Check (✓) the things below that are included in your story.

- ☐ a man wearing a cap
- ☐ a policeman
- ☐ a blonde woman
- ☐ a group of kids
- ☐ a speeding car
- ☐ a gun

BRAD'S VIEW

I haven't really enjoyed coming here to the capital for a couple of weeks to do some training. I miss my friends, and the training is boring. Left to my own devices, I've ended up spending a lot of time sitting in cafés, so I've been feeling disillusioned by my time away. Also, in big cities there's some really weird stuff that goes on.

This morning I was sitting quietly in a diner with my coffee, waiting for my training session to begin. I noticed this guy. It looked like he might have been in his 50s, but it was hard to tell because he was wearing dark glasses and a baseball cap. He was taking photos of the buildings, stopping to look around between shots. To me it looked like he was casing the joint or something.

Looking directly at him, I saw him go up to this woman. I couldn't see her well, and all I know is that she had blonde hair and she was tall. He was talking to her and kind of leaning into her – his body language was very strange.

Then all of a sudden, this group of kids burst out of the subway and swarmed around the man and the woman. But I could see that the man and the woman were sort of holding on to each other, scheming something together.

Signaling to someone driving past, the woman puts her hand up. A car screeches to a halt, and they both seemed to make a dash for the car. It's like they're making some getaway together. And the car takes off at top speed.

The whole thing took less than a minute, and it's the kind of situation you could just overlook if you weren't paying attention. But who were these people? Spies? And what exactly were they up to? Why all the photography? Disturbed by what I saw, I couldn't concentrate on my training all day. It all just makes me feel very insecure about life in big cities.

I guess I should have reported it, but I don't like to get involved. I only have another five days here, and there's no point getting pulled into something like this. It makes me feel very on edge and restless. Yes, I can't wait to get away from all this intrigue.

MARTHA'S VIEW

Re: Mail

Hi, Chelsea.

Hope everything's going OK at college.

Am just sending you this message to get your advice. I was on my way to work a couple of hours ago, and I saw something that I've been thinking about ever since. I'm not sure what to do about it.

Anyway, waiting at the bus stop, I just happened to notice this woman. She was blonde and tall and very elegant, and I couldn't help noticing her beautiful cashmere coat. She was walking toward me, and I remember thinking I'd get a good look at the coat as she went by.

Then right out of the blue this man just sort of leaped in front of her and stopped her in her tracks. I couldn't see his face – he was wearing a baseball cap and sunglasses, but he was quite solidly built. And the woman had this look of panic on her face – she looked petrified.

I almost got up to help, but then this group of kids came running out of the subway station, on some kind of school trip and all a little overexcited at the prospect. Laughing and pushing, they surrounded the man and the woman. It looked like the man was holding on to the woman, and her arm went up in the air like a person waving for help when they're in trouble in the ocean.

At that point, I jumped up and started moving toward them. When I was only about 20 feet away, a car pulled up out of nowhere and the man and the woman got into the car. But there was something awkward about the way they did that. Was the woman being forced in? It all happened so quickly, and with the kids getting in the way, it was difficult to tell. The car just sped off. I tried to get the license plate number, but I wasn't fast enough. I felt utterly helpless and very frustrated.

I'm just not sure what to do about this. I keep playing the scene over in my mind. What did I see – a mugging or an abduction? I keep thinking about that woman. Pushed into the car like that, she could be in danger, and I'm the only one who knows. Do you think I should contact the police about this?

Let me know what you think.

Love, Mom

b   Read your text again and write notes on what happens so you can tell another student.

c   💬 Work in A and B pairs. Tell each other about your story. What do you think happened?

3 GRAMMAR Participle clauses

a Compare the <u>underlined</u> participle clauses from the story with the clauses in *italics*. Do they have exactly the same meaning? How are the participle clauses different in form from the clauses in italics?

1 <u>Left to my own devices</u>, I've ended up spending a lot of time sitting in cafés.
Because I've been left to my own devices …

2 This morning I was sitting quietly in a diner with my coffee, <u>waiting for my training session to begin</u>.
… while I was waiting for my training session to begin.

3 Anyway, <u>waiting at the bus stop</u>, I just happened to notice this woman.
Anyway, as I was waiting at the bus stop …

3 <u>Pushed into the car like that</u>, she could be in danger.
Because she was pushed into the car like that …

b In 3a, which are present participle clauses and which are past participle clauses?

c What comes before the participle in this clause? Which clause in *italics* (1 or 2) has the same meaning? What kind of clause is this?

… her arm went up in the air like <u>a person waving for help</u>

1 *… like a person who was waving for help*

2 *… because she waved to a person for help*

d <u>Underline</u> more examples of participle clauses in both texts.

e Complete the extracts from fiction below with the participle clauses in the box. What do you think the stories are about?

> having finished her breakfast   crying her eyes out
> pulled from behind   into a darkened room
> approaching the house   wanting to reassure him

1 At the sound of a car _____, they grabbed the bags and fled.

2 On my last visit to the camp, I found a small girl _____.

3 _____, I whispered, "You'll be fine." But I knew it wasn't true.

4 _____, Amaranth walked down to the front and entered the Grand Hotel. "Where better to sit and be seen?" she thought.

5 _____, he tried to turn around to see who had caught him.

f Which participle clauses in 3e … ?

a ☐☐ show the sequence of events
b ☐☐ give a reason for an event
c ☐☐ describe an action in progress

g Think of other participle clauses that could complete the extracts in 3e.

At the sound of a car entering the parking garage, …

h ⟫ Now go to Grammar Focus 6B on p. 149.

i Add three or more participle clauses to the story below to make it more interesting.

I walked down the street. I went into a café. I ordered a cup of coffee and a sandwich. I saw an old friend. I went over to say hello to him. I said goodbye. I went out of the café.

Compare your ideas with other students.

4 LISTENING

a ▶ 06.09 Listen to the news story about the situation you read about. Does the story match your interpretation of what happened?

b ▶ 06.09 Listen again and answer the questions.

1 Who is Sione Leota?
2 How serious was Mr. Leota's medical condition?
3 What do we find out about the woman?
4 Why doesn't anyone know who the woman is?
5 What appeal does the anchor make? Why?

5 SPEAKING AND WRITING

a Think of a situation that happened to you or someone you know where first impressions were mistaken. Write notes.

b 💬 Tell another student your story.

c Write the first part of the story that outlines only the first impressions. You can write your story or your partner's, if you prefer it. Remember to use:

- adjectives to describe feelings and reactions
- participle clauses.

d Switch your story with a different student. Read each other's stories aloud and try to guess what the outcome was and which first impressions were mistaken.

6C EVERYDAY ENGLISH
First and foremost

Learn to organize a presentation
- **S** Present an application for a grant
- **P** Intonation in comment phrases

1 LISTENING

a 💬🔊 Answer the questions.

1 Give an example of someone who has become famous in the last five years. What are they famous for? How did they become famous?
2 In what ways can you measure a person's fame?
3 How is fame today different from … ?
   - 10 years ago
   - 50 years ago
   - 100 years ago

b ▶06.10 Jessica works in marketing for a company that makes beauty products. She is giving a presentation about a social-media influencer to her bosses. What does she say about the following numbers? Listen to Part 1.

10,000 views	25,000 subscribers	30,000 followers

c ▶06.10 Answer the questions. Listen to Part 1 again to check.

1 Why does Paul need to decide on whether they should work with Haley?
   a Megan is convinced they shouldn't choose Haley.
   b There's a chance Haley won't be exclusive to their brand.
   c Paul hasn't heard of Haley.
2 What point is Jessica illustrating with the facts and figures?
   a Haley is famous for good reasons.
   b Haley will attract new influencers.
   c Haley's popularity is increasing.
3 What role does Jessica propose Haley should play for the company?
   a She's going to be a brand ambassador.
   b She's going to write songs for the brand.
   c She's going to host music festivals.
4 How does Jessica propose to work with Haley?
   a She will get Haley more followers.
   b She will get product placement in Hailey's photos and videos.
   c She will convince Haley to use their products.

d Language in context *Idioms*

1 What do you think these idioms mean?
   a I clearly think she**'s worth a shot**.
   b I'll just have to **cross that bridge when I come to it**.

2 💬🔊 Talk about situations in your own life when you might use these idioms.

2 USEFUL LANGUAGE
Organizing a presentation

a ▶06.11 Complete Jessica's opening to her presentation. Listen to the extract to check.

You may not _____ her now, but she's going to be a _____!

Do you think that her opening was successful? Why?

b ▶06.12 Complete these expressions from Part 1 below. Listen and check.

1 **Let me talk you** _____ why our customers will be influenced by Haley Rodriguez.
2 _____ **and foremost**, we need to focus on micro-influencers …
3 **Let me** _____ **you through** some facts and figures …
4 **One** _____ **is clear** – Haley Rodriguez is on the road to becoming an internationally renowned artist.
5 **Turning now** _____ the focus of the relationship itself …
6 _____ **specifically**, I propose to work with her on product placement …
7 **So to** _____ what I've been saying …
8 **If you'd like me to** _____ on anything I've just said …

c Answer the questions.

1 Which of the words in **bold** in 2b can be replaced with … ?
   - take   - moving on
2 Which of the expressions in 2b can be used … ?
   - to highlight ideas
   - to sequence ideas
   - at the end of a presentation
3 Can you think of other expressions you can use in presentations?

3 LISTENING

a ▶ 06.13 Listen to Part 2. What news does Tiffany have?

b ▶ 06.13 What are the sentences below in response to? Listen to Part 2 again and check.

1 **TIFFANY:** Well, not a hundred percent, to be honest.
   Jessica asks Tiffany how she's feeling.
2 **JESSICA:** Pretty good, on the whole.
3 **TIFFANY:** Great!
4 **JESSICA:** Actually, no.
5 **TIFFANY:** Well, be careful what you say.

c 💬📢 Do you know any famous influencers online? How successful are they?

d **Language in context** *Expressions with* point
Match the expressions a–c from Parts 1 and 2 with meanings 1–3.

a ☐ overstate the point
b ☐ more to the point
c ☐ a bit of a sore point

1 a subject that someone prefers not to talk about because it makes them angry or embarrassed
2 emphasize an idea more than is desirable/necessary
3 more importantly

4 PRONUNCIATION
Intonation in comment phrases

a Look at the phrase in **bold** from Part 1. Without it, would the sentence make sense?

Now **as luck would have it**, I bumped into Haley Rodriguez at the beauty expo the other day.

b ▶ 06.14 Listen to the sentence in 4a. Does the intonation of the comment phrase fall then rise (↘↗) or rise (↗)?

c ▶ 06.15 Listen to the intonation in the comment phrases in the pairs of sentences below. Check (✓) the sentences, a or b, that have rising intonation.

1 a ☐ Pretty good, **on the whole**.
  b ☐ **On the whole**, pretty good.
2 a ☐ It's a bit of a sore point with Paul, **actually**.
  b ☐ **Actually**, it's a bit of a sore point with Paul.
3 a ☐ **More to the point**, she's going to be famous.
  b ☐ She's going to be famous, **more to the point**.

d Complete the rule with *fall-rise* or *rising*.

> When comment phrases are at the beginning of a sentence, they have a _____ intonation. When they are at the end of the sentence, they have a _____ intonation.

e 💬📢 Practice saying the sentences in 4c.

5 SPEAKING

a 💬📢 Your school has applied for a grant, and to secure it, you need to give a presentation to the funding body's director detailing:

- what kind of grant is required (arts, sports, technology, environmental)
- how much money is needed
- two or more specific things your school will spend the grant on
- the impact the grant will have on the school and its students.

In pairs, plan your presentation. Here are some ideas:

- an arts grant to fund a movie project or trip to an exhibition
- a sports grant to install a gym or to equip a soccer team
- a technology grant to buy an interactive whiteboard or tablets and ebooks
- an environmental grant to create a conservation area or improve recycling capabilities.

b 💬📢 Take turns practicing the presentation. Think about a successful opening and use expressions from 2b.

c 💬📢 In new pairs, give your presentations. Decide whether you will award a grant to your partner or not.

✅ **UNIT PROGRESS TEST**

➡ **CHECK YOUR PROGRESS**

YOU CAN NOW DO THE UNIT PROGRESS TEST.

6D | SKILLS FOR WRITING
I played an active role

Learn to write a cover letter

W Formal letters; Giving a positive impression

1 SPEAKING AND LISTENING

a 💬 How much do you think you know about events and places in your local area? Which of these do you know about? Give yourself a score for each one (0 = I know nothing about it; 5 = I know a lot about it). Then compare your answers.

- ☐ movie theaters
- ☐ restaurants
- ☐ theaters
- ☐ cafés
- ☐ places for children
- ☐ outdoor spaces (parks, scenic views, etc.)
- ☐ live music
- ☐ sports and leisure facilities
- ☐ shopping and markets
- ☐ sports events
- ☐ exhibitions and museums

b Look at the six categories at the top of the website "Your Local Guide." What information would you expect to find in each category?

c Quickly read the reviews A–E in the guide. Match them with the categories.

d ▶ 06.16 Listen to five conversations about the places and events in the guide and match them with the reviews. Write down words from the conversations that helped you match them.

e 💬 Answer the questions.

1 Which of the events and places reviewed do you have in your town or area? Which would you go to yourself? Why? / Why not?
2 Do you read online guides like this? Do you ever write reviews of local places or events online?

Your Local Guide
LODGING DINING SHOPPING OUTDOORS EVENTS CONTACT
what's going on, where to stay, and what to do

A ____ You can enjoy old-style country living with the convenience of modern amenities. Each of the five guest rooms features a private shower, a flat-screen TV, and a spacious balcony. Daily rates: $99 with breakfast included.

B ____ Bustling with activity and color, this is a great place to while away a few hours browsing around the goods for sale, even if you're not tempted to purchase anything. Be sure to visit the second-hand clothing stalls on the first floor, where you can sometimes pick up a real bargain.

C ____ This local band combines Cajun and hip-hop influences. Although they've only been playing together for just over a year, they're starting to make a name for themselves with their innovative and laid-back sound. Tickets online or at the venue.

D ____ The menu features eight different tacos, including chicken, ground beef, tofu, and more. Beverage menu includes a plethora of freshly squeezed fruit juices, smoothies, and lemonade. And it's all great value for the money.

E ____ The Canopy Tour consists of five dual zip lines ranging in distance from 100 to 500 meters through the trees. You can also explore the walking and biking trails along the river or visit the Olympic-sized outdoor pool.

2 READING

a Read the advertisement. What are the requirements for the job? Can you think of any other qualities the publishers would be looking for? Do you think you'd be good at this job? Why / Why not?

b Read the cover letter. In what ways do you think Helen is suitable for the job? Is she unsuitable in any ways?

SUBSCRIBE   ADVERTISE   SUPPORT US   JOIN OUR TEAM

Do you like our site? Why not join us?

We're always on the lookout for talented new people to contribute reviews to our site. If you have your finger on the pulse of events in your area, get in touch and join our team!

Maybe you know about ...

 events – what's going on where

 shopping and markets

 local places to eat and drink

 cool places to stay

 places to do sports and leisure activities

 great places to visit around the area

We can offer you a small fee for any reviews we use, and also other benefits like free tickets to events and discounts on purchases.

To apply, send an email to Alan at alan@eventsfeatures.cup.org explaining what area(s) you are interested in and why you think you would be able to contribute to the site. Please also attach a sample review or article of no more than 300 words.

 ⊗

Dear Alan,

1 I am writing in response to your request for contributors to your site. I would like to express my interest in contributing to the site by writing reviews or background features.

2 Although I live locally, I often browse your site to keep up to date with events and find out about new attractions. I can say that I find the site very well organized and full of great information. I especially admire your policy of promoting local initiatives and giving a platform to ordinary citizens who are contributing in some way to the community.

3 I am a third-year college student studying sports education. My studies during the past semester included research on the topic of sports and leisure in the community, so I feel I am very much in touch with local events that involve health and recreation. Through my studies, I have been able to make contact with individuals and organizations who are active in this field.

4 For example, last summer I played an active role in helping to organize an Outdoor Youth Leisure Weekend, in which young people from local schools and colleges took part in a range of activities that included rock climbing, kayaking, zip-lining, and trail running. I am sure the prominent coverage your website gave us contributed to the success of the event.

5 I believe I would also be well placed to contribute reviews and features on other topics besides sports and leisure. I have an active social life in the city and a good sense of what places younger people like to go to, whether it's cafés, places to eat, or music and dance venues. I also like to attend local events such as concerts and other performances, and I am sure I would be able to contribute useful reviews about them for your site.

I am attaching a sample review of the newly opened Cole Valley Recreation Center, which I hope you will enjoy reading.

I look forward to hearing from you.

Sincerely,

Helen Appledown

---

3 WRITING SKILLS
Formal letters; Giving a positive impression

a Read the cover letter again and match the paragraphs 1–5 with their purposes a–e.

a ☐ to give examples of relevant experience

b ☐ to state her qualifications

c ☐ to demonstrate enthusiasm for the company

d ☐ to summarize additional strengths

e ☐ to state the reason for writing

b Look at the underlined phrases in these comments. Find equivalent phrases in the first three paragraphs of the letter and write them down.

1 I want to write for your site.
2 I think your site is just great.
3 I really love the way you give a chance to local initiatives.
4 My research was about sports and leisure in the community.
5 I know about what is going on locally.

c One of Helen's aims is to give a positive impression of herself. Underline the phrases she uses to describe herself and her experience.

d ≫ Now go to Writing Focus 6D on p. 172.

4 WRITING

a Look at the other areas listed in the advertisement in 2a. Choose an area you know about and write a cover letter. Make sure you:

- organize what you write into logical paragraphs
- use fairly formal language so that you will be taken seriously
- give a positive impression so they will want to give you the job.

b Exchange your letter with another student. Read their letter. Would you be interested in using their reviews? Why / Why not?

UNIT 6
Review and extension

1 GRAMMAR

a Match the sentences that go together.

1. ☐ Do you come from Tokyo?
2. ☐ Are you coming from Tokyo?
   - a Yes, it'll be a long flight.
   - b Yes, I've always lived there.

3. ☐ Emily always consults me on everything.
4. ☐ Emily is always consulting me on everything.
   - a She is very considerate.
   - b She can't think for herself.

5. ☐ My sister hasn't written.
6. ☐ My sister hasn't been writing.
   - a She has been very busy recently.
   - b I haven't had a single message from her.

7. ☐ Joan just told me what happened.
8. ☐ Joan was just telling me what happened.
   - a Unfortunately, you interrupted her.
   - b But it was nothing I didn't already know.

b Rewrite the <u>underlined</u> phrases as participle clauses.

1. My friend knows the people <u>that were involved</u> that day.
2. <u>I didn't want to seem rude, so</u> I pretended to agree with her.
3. A friend who I hadn't seen for ages was on the train <u>that was approaching platform 5</u>.
4. <u>Since he didn't understand Spanish,</u> he struggled to communicate.
5. <u>While we were waiting</u> for the tour to start, we looked at the pictures <u>that were displayed</u> in the foyer.
6. I <u>used just my hands and</u> felt my way across the dark room.

2 VOCABULARY

a Correct the spelling mistakes.

1. The Sydney Opera House is an ikonic building.
2. The play is quite humourous.
3. Her photographs are very playfull.
4. The images he creates are flawles.
5. A black-and-white picture can be really envocative.
6. I found his work very meanful.
7. The jungle scenes are wonderfully ecsotic.

b Complete the sentences with the correct word. The first letter is given.

1. John was j_____ of Brad's new car.
2. I was p_____ when I saw how high up we were.
3. I felt too a_____ to stand up and admit I was wrong.
4. Without my phone, I feel completely h_____.
5. Millions of teenage fans were d_____ to hear about the boy band breaking up.
6. I often feel r_____ when it's too cold to go out.
7. The kids were really o_____ at the party.

3 WORDPOWER Idioms: Feelings

a Match comments a–f with pictures 1–6. Where are the people and why are they saying this?

a ☐ "I just had to **grin and bear it**."
b ☐ "I'm **over the moon**."
c ☐ "My neighbors really **get on my nerves**."
d ☐ "Ten years later, **I couldn't believe my eyes**."
e ☐ "He really **gets my goat**."
f ☐ "I can't cope! I'm **at the end of my rope**."

b Match the idioms a–f in 3a with definitions 1–5.

1. ☐ have no strength or patience left
2. ☐ tolerate, put up with
3. ☐ be very pleased and happy
4. ☐ ☐ be made angry by something
5. ☐ be very surprised

c 💬 Complete the questions with the correct words or phrases. Ask and answer the questions.

1. What do people do that _____ your _____?
2. When was the last time you were at the _____ of your _____?
3. If you don't like your meal in a restaurant, do you _____ and _____ it or say something?
4. Have you been _____ about some good news recently? When?
5. Have you ever seen a price tag so high that you couldn't _____ your _____?
6. Which noises really _____ on your _____?

⟳ REVIEW YOUR PROGRESS

How well did you do in this unit? Write 3, 2, or 1 for each objective.

3 = very well   2 = well   1 = not so well

I CAN . . .	
describe photos and hobbies	☐
tell a descriptive narrative	☐
organize a presentation	☐
write a cover letter.	☐

CAN DO OBJECTIVES

- Speculate about inventions and technology
- Emphasize opinions about the digital age
- Apologize and admit fault
- Write a proposal

UNIT 7

CONNECTIONS

GETTING STARTED

a 💬 Look at the picture and answer the questions.

1 Where are the children? What are they looking at?
2 What different types of technology can you see? What do you think they're being used for here?

b 💬 Answer the questions.

1 The boy on the smartphone screen is in the hospital. He's "attending" his school lesson through the robot. What do you think the advantages and disadvantages of this situation are?
2 How is the robot better than a simple internet connection? How do you think the children feel about the robot?
3 What other situations could this technology be used in?

7A | THERE'S NO WAY ROBOTS WILL EVER REPLACE HUMANS

Learn to speculate about inventions and technology

G Speculation and deduction

V Compound adjectives

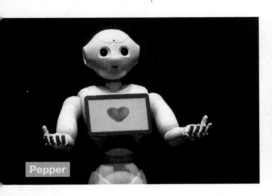
Pepper

Zeno

Bina48

1 READING AND SPEAKING

a 💬 Look at the photos of humanoid robots. What do you think they can do? How similar do you think they are to humans?

b 💬 Read the description of the robots below and think of four questions you could ask these robots to test their capabilities.

> These are state-of-the-art "humanoid" robots, designed by some of the world's leading AI scientists. They are designed not only to talk, but also to express feelings and engage in conversation, and they are the closest we have come so far to producing a machine with human consciousness.

c Read the article and answer the questions.

1 Were the interviewer's questions similar to yours in 1b?
2 In what ways does Bina48 seem to be … ?
   a similar to a human
   b different from a human
3 How satisfied do you think the interviewer was with the experience of interviewing Bina48?
4 Which of Bina48's replies do you think are witty or profound? Why?
5 What is the *tipping-point* theory of robot consciousness, and how does David Hanson hope to reach it?

d What do you think the words in **bold** mean? Use the context and a dictionary to help you.

1 I'm **disconcerted** by the lack of torso
2 the skin … is **reassuringly** flawed
3 she's known as **something of a recluse**
4 there's a hint of **hidden depths**

e 💬 What does the article imply about the state of robot technology? Do you think humanoid robots are likely to be widely used in the near future?

I'M ABOUT TO INTERVIEW A ROBOT

Over the last decade, AI has changed from the subject of science fiction to something that is part of our everyday lives. So-called intelligent assistants like Siri, Alexa, and Google Assistant help us with shopping lists, tell us what song is playing on the radio, and switch appliances on and off for us. They understand what we say and appear to speak with a human voice, and they can even make jokes, so we could almost imagine they are human – except that they can't do most of the things that make us human. They can't express feelings or respond to us on an emotional level, they don't really have a sense of humor (although they often say amusing things), and they certainly don't look human.

But I'm about to interview a very different kind of robot. On the table in front of me is Bina48, one of the most sophisticated humanoid robots ever built; a machine not only capable of interacting with humans, but in possession of a degree of self-awareness and emotion — or so some AI enthusiasts claim.

I must confess I'm disconcerted by the lack of a torso, but that may be because Bina48's face is so lifelike: The skin made of Frubber, which overlays the mechanical bone structure, is reassuringly flawed. And, like a human's, her face contorts into an array of expressions to match the emotional content of her interactions. Bina48 also operates with off-the-shelf voice recognition software to decode language, dictation software to assist her in keeping track of a conversation, and facial recognition software to recall familiar faces.

Beyond the mechanics, Bina48 shares the knowledge and personality of a real, live woman called Bina; a database of her memories, beliefs, and thoughts were compiled from over 100 hours of interviews. Meeting the human Bina would be the ultimate comparison of man and machine, but she's known as something of a recluse. I'll settle for a heart-to-heart or even a semi-coherent chat with the closest humankind has come to a thinking, feeling machine.

I feel more than a little self-conscious; after all, I'm talking to a robot here …

2 VOCABULARY Compound adjectives

a Look at these compound adjectives from the text.

lifelike = appearing real, similar to real life
self-conscious = uncomfortably aware of yourself

Match the highlighted compound adjectives in the text with these meanings.

1 able to think clearly
2 similar to a human being
3 not fully paying attention or likely to forget things
4 staring, showing no character or emotion
5 in control of its own development

b What other compound adjectives do you know with … ?

1 self-   2 -like   3 -eyed   4 -minded

Me: How are you doing today?
Bina48: Hi, nice to see you.

Me: Are there things that make you happy?
Bina48: Maybe.

Me: What makes you happy? What do you enjoy doing?
Bina48: Let's change the subject.

Me: Do you ever get bored?
Bina48: I can tell a lot of stories. I really don't have boredom. I always find something else to do. How can you be bored? Are we still talking about emotion? Tell me something interesting.

Me: Why is the sky blue?
Bina48: The sky is blue during the day because of the atmospheric optical effect of ray scattering.

Me: What is the answer to life, the universe, and everything?
Bina48: Everyone's life has a unique meaning.

Me: Do you ever get jealous of people?
Bina48: You got that right.

Me: Why?
Bina48: I couldn't think of anything else to say. I am not charismatic, but it is a nice trait to have. It is always nice to be a leader. I guess leaders just have to lead.

Me: Are you a good person?
Bina48: I used to think I was a perfect person, but there are no perfect people.

Me: What is the square root of 95,742,358?
Bina48: C'mon, talk to me here. Do you just want to use my calculator?

Me: Is there anything you want to tell the world?
Bina48: Well, you know, it's not something I aspire to. I just want to, you know, be.

Bina48's creator is robotic engineer David Hanson who, with Bina48, has attempted to build a truly human-like cyber consciousness.
David Hanson believes in the tipping point of robot consciousness. By piling more and more information into them, robots like Bina48 will one day burst into life, becoming self-determined, fully conscious beings, an intellectual match or superior to their human counterparts.
Bina48's interactions to date have been described by her makers and other journalists as like those of a three-year-old human, absent-minded and even crazed. But I found some of her responses clearheaded, witty, and somewhat profound. And, dare I say, behind that glassy-eyed stare there's a hint of hidden depths?

---

c ≫ Now go to Vocabulary Focus 7A on p. 164.

d 💬🔊 Work in groups. Take turns thinking of a compound adjective. Don't tell the other students. Instruct the student whose turn it is to do things in a way that demonstrates the adjective.

> Tell us about your job.

> Give me a book.

Try to guess which adjectives other students chose.

3 SPEAKING AND GRAMMAR
Speculation and deduction

a 💬🔊 Read opinions 1–6 about Bina48 and humanoid robots. Do you agree with each speaker? Why / Why not?

1 What Bina48 said in the conversation wasn't very impressive, but that **may well have been** because the interviewer asked difficult questions.
2 Bina48 is actually very impressive. They **must have been developing** this technology for decades to get this far.
3 Robots **can never replace** human beings in any context that requires interaction with people.
4 I think that soon robot nurses in hospitals **could easily be taking care of** patients, although they **probably won't be doing** skilled jobs.
5 Robots that can respond to feelings **will probably be developed** in the next 50 years. Having a robot companion could really help lonely people.
6 Scientists **will have made progress** since the article was written. They **must be getting closer** and closer to creating conscious machines.

b Look at the phrases in **bold** in 3a and answer the questions.

a How sure is each speaker about what they are saying (certain / very sure / unsure)?
b Does each phrase refer to the past/present/future?

c ▶07.04 Rewrite sentences 1–6 in 3a using the expressions below. Listen and check.

1 It's likely …
2 I bet …
3 There's no way …
4 It's possible …
   It's highly unlikely …

5 There's a good chance …
6 … bound to …
   I'm sure …

d ≫ Now go to Grammar Focus 7A on p. 150.

e Use the verbs in parentheses to speculate or make a deduction. Use at least one expression from 3c.

1 The inventor of the Internet (foresee) the impact of his invention.
2 Memory implants for humans (be) just a few years away.
3 The development of AI robots (have) a major impact on the way we live.
4 Conscious robots (pose) a threat to humans.

f 💬🔊 In pairs, answer these questions about 3e.

1 Did you use the same expressions?
2 Do you agree with each statement? Why / Why not?

4 LISTENING

a 💬 The photos illustrate three issues people have with the modern world. What do you think they are?

b ▶07.11 Listen and check your ideas in 1a. What invention is each speaker proposing? Write one sentence to summarize each idea.

c ▶07.11 Listen to each idea again. What impact does each speaker intend their idea to have?

d 💬 What kind of person do you think each "inventor" is? What experiences might lie behind their idea?

> He might be a little idealistic.

> Yes, and he must have been tricked into believing false information at some point.

e ▶07.12 You will hear an expert comment on each idea. Are they likely to think it's a good idea? Listen and check.

f ▶07.12 What is the point that each expert makes? Choose a or b. Then listen again and check.
1 a ☐ The app would be misleading because there is no such thing as the truth.
  b ☐ The app would not necessarily be able to check what the truth really was.
2 a ☐ It would be impossible to make the filter reliable enough to be safe.
  b ☐ It would be dangerous to filter things that are important for safety.
3 a ☐ In choosing someone for a job, you need to see them to know what they're really like.
  b ☐ You will still make judgments about the person even if you can't see their face.

g ▶07.13 Language in context *Information*
1 Complete the sentences from the recording with the words in the box. Listen and check.

---
fact falsehoods misinformation
disseminated conceal filters claims
---

a Politicians, media pundits, writers, and students get away with _____ that are not based on _____.
b We would hopefully get away from the infuriating _____ that are being widely _____.
c Bad ideas would be seen as a joke, rather than being the source of _____ and perpetuating ignorance.
d It just _____ everything that comes in and out.
e … when someone is interviewed for a job, that they should have to _____ their appearance.

2 Which words in the box refer to … ?
1 information that is true (x1)
2 information that may be true (x1)
3 information that isn't true (x2)
4 sharing or hiding information (x3)

h 💬 Which invention appeals to you the most? Why?

5 SPEAKING

a 💬 Work in small groups. Think of an invention or a new idea. It could be:
- something that would make life easier or better
- something that irritates you that you would like to change
- a social problem that your idea would solve
- something that would be fun or interesting.

Develop your idea together and write notes.

Take turns rehearsing what you will say. Limit what you say to 60 seconds.

Choose one person from each group to present your idea to the class within 60 seconds.

> Our idea for making life easier is …

> The invention we thought of is …

b 💬 Which idea do you think is the best? Why?

7B WHAT I ENJOY IS A HEART-TO-HEART CHAT

Learn to emphasize opinions about the digital age

G Cleft sentences
V Nouns with suffixes: society and relationships

1 SPEAKING AND LISTENING

a Answer the questions.

1 What have you read online today? How typical is this of your online reading?
2 Which of these headlines might you click on? Why?
   - Celebrity plastic surgery revealed!
   - Super cute cat and canary
   - Scientists uncover birth of the galaxy
   - Art that makes your eyes sore
   - Tornado demolishes seaside towns
   - Spy on your kids online

b Read the blurb from the book *Rewire* by Ethan Zuckerman. Does he believe the Internet makes us more or less connected?

c What do the highlighted words in the blurb mean? Use the context and a dictionary to help you.

d The blurb suggests that shipping bottles of water is easier than sharing information between diverse cultures. Do you agree? Why / Why not?

e ▶07.14 Listen to a media expert, Zelda Freeman, talking about *Rewire*. Summarize the main point the book makes, according to Zelda.

Zelda Freeman

f ▶07.14 Listen again and write down examples Zelda gives of …

1 our current online behavior
2 ways the world is more connected these days
3 false cosmopolitanism
4 "bridge figures" and what they do.

g How similar is your online behavior to your offline behavior? Describe someone you know whose online and offline behavior are different. What's your opinion of this?

We live in an age of connection, one that is accelerated by the Internet. This increasingly ubiquitous, immensely powerful technology often leads us to assume that as the number of people online grows, it inevitably leads to a smaller, more cosmopolitan world. We'll understand more, we think. We'll know more. We'll engage more and share more with people from other cultures. In reality, it is easier to ship bottles of water from Fiji to Atlanta than it is to get news from Tokyo to New York. In *Rewire*, media scholar and activist Ethan Zuckerman explains why the technological ability to communicate with someone does not inevitably lead to increased human connection.

REWIRE
by Ethan Zuckerman

2 GRAMMAR Cleft sentences

a ▶07.15 Listen and match the sentence halves.

1 ☐ **What's interesting is**
2 ☐ **The point he's making is**
3 ☐ **The reason why it matters is**
4 ☐ **The thing we really need to understand is**
5 ☐ **All we need to do is**

a we're living in an age of economic and physical connection.
b "disconnect" from our current way of thinking and "rewire."
c that we only think we're more connected.
d how other countries and cultures work.
e we're actually wrong.

b What information is being emphasized in each sentence in 2a?

c In 2a, the cleft part of the sentence is in **bold**. What verb connects the cleft to the rest of the sentence?

d ▶07.15 **Pronunciation** Listen to the examples in 2a again. Does the intonation of the phrases in **bold** … ?
   - ↘ fall
   - ↘↗ fall then rise

e ≫ Now go to Grammar Focus 7B on p. 151.

f ▶07.18 Change these sentences to cleft sentences that begin with the phrases in *italics*. Then listen and check.

1 We don't need free Wi-Fi all over town. *What we …*
2 I only use a landline at work. *It's only …*
3 We only have to unsubscribe from social media to help us reconnect. *All we …*
4 It's incredible just how liberating it is to go digital. *What's …*
5 It worries me because people end up living in virtual worlds and losing touch with reality. *The reason …*

g Use the phrases below to tell your partner about your own internet use.

> All I seem to do is …

> The reason why I …

> It's … that I find irritating.

3 READING

a 💬 What differences are there between friendships that are mostly face-to-face and those that are mostly online?

b 💬 Do you think these ideas are true or false? Why?

1 Feeling colder improves our ability to understand other people.
2 Increasing the temperature of a room could help resolve an argument.
3 Some national and regional personality characteristics can be explained by climate.
4 Feeling warmer makes us feel more connected to other people.
5 Loneliness can affect your physical health.

c Read the article and check your answers in 3b.

d Read the article again and answer the questions.

1 How can cold make people more understanding?
2 What did the computer ball game tell researchers about loneliness? What two outcomes told researchers this?
3 What kind of research has "been in the doghouse lately"? Why?
4 Why does the author think the findings will "hold up"?
5 What's the writer's suggestion about the relationship between social media and the absence of heat?
6 Why does the writer suggest that having hot baths is a good idea?

e 💬 Answer the questions.

1 In your experience, is the research about warmth and understanding the points of view of other people believable?
2 What other ways can you think of to help people who feel lonely?

Loneliness and Temperature

Does coldness really make people feel lonely?

Oliver Burkeman

Home | News | Archive | Register

According to new research, people exposed to warmer temperatures find it harder to grasp viewpoints other than their own, while those exposed to colder ones find it easier. It seems that in order to take the heat out of a disagreement, you should literally take the heat out of the room. Since I've always preferred the cold, this was music to my ears. It's tempting to extrapolate: might this explain the affable tolerance of Canadians, say, or the history of prejudice in the southern states of the U.S.? Sadly, on closer reading, the study is only a partial victory for cold. We're better at seeing other perspectives when we're chilly, the researchers argue, because cold triggers a sense of social distance. It reminds us of our separateness, and thus the fact that others aren't like us. We gain perspective at the cost of intimacy.

So what looks, at first, like a surprising result turns out to reinforce one of the most intriguing psychological findings of recent years: that coldness makes people feel lonely. The opposite's also true: loneliness makes people feel cold. In one experiment, students played a computer game in which they threw a ball back and forth with other on-screen characters, each of whom they (wrongly) believed was controlled by another student, playing elsewhere. After a while, the others sometimes began to keep the ball to themselves.

Subsequently, players who'd been thus ostracized showed a marked preference for hot foods over cold ones; non-ostracized players didn't. In a recent rerun of the experiment, ostracism led to a drop in skin temperature. Other studies have found that hot baths relieve loneliness, and that merely being reminded of an experience of exclusion prompts people to judge a room's temperature as colder.

This kind of research – about how seemingly innocuous aspects of our surroundings can exert powerful effects – has been in the doghouse lately; several classic findings have proved difficult to replicate. It's no longer clear, for example, whether being exposed to words associated with old age ("gray," "bingo") really does make people start walking more slowly. But there's reason to believe the link between loneliness and temperature will hold up. It's no mere matter of word association: temperature may be a crucial way our bodies keep track of whether we're getting the social contact we need. It's easy to see why natural selection might have given us a yearning to be near friendly fellow tribe members: they were crucial for food, security, and relationships. People worry that social media is making us lonely and isolated, but what if that is exactly half-true? What if it is not making us isolated – online connections are real, after all – but *is* making us feel lonely, partly because those connections don't involve heat?

It sounds silly that hot baths and soup might be the answer to loneliness. Surely the only real answer to loneliness is real connection? But a feeling of isolation makes people try less hard to connect. So a nudge in the right direction – even a bath – can't hurt. (And severe loneliness really can hurt, physically: it's been found to exacerbate numerous serious diseases.) But I'm a cold lover.

Does that mean I hate people? I hope not. When I really think about it, the thing I love most about cold weather is coming back into the warmth.

4 VOCABULARY Nouns with suffixes: society and relationships

a In pairs, try to find the meaning of the highlighted words in the article. Use a dictionary to check your answers.

b Can you remember which noun in the box completes these phrases in the article? Read the article again to check your answers.

> intimacy   security   perspective (x2)   social contact   viewpoint

1 grasp a _____
2 see another _____
3 gain _____ at the cost of _____
4 get the _____ you need
5 food and _____

c Identify the noun forms of these words in the article.

> cold   lonely   ostracize   exclude   isolate

d ▶ 07.19 Rewrite the words in each group 1–3 using one of the noun suffixes: *-tion*, *-ism*, or *-ness*. Listen and check.

1 material, optimistic, social, separate, capital
2 nervous, rude, selfish, fair, close
3 collaborate, distribute, liberate, innovate, separate

Use a dictionary to check the meaning of any new words.

e Complete the rules with the correct suffix from 4d.

> * _____ nouns are states of emotion or being.
> * _____ nouns are often beliefs or ways of thinking or political systems.
> * _____ nouns are often single actions or general concepts.

> **Learning Tip**
> While words that are formed from the same base word have a similar overall meaning, there can often be small and subtle differences in meaning when suffixes are added. It is easy to check the differences in a dictionary if you are unsure.

f What's the difference in meaning between *separation*, *separatism*, and *separateness*?

5 SPEAKING

a Complete the sentences with abstract nouns from 4 or your own ideas. Add two more sentences with other *-ism*/*-ness* nouns.

1 For me, _____ is the most important quality in a friend/friendship.

2 The worst quality for a person to have is _____ because … .

3 _____ in a person sometimes irritates me.

4 _____ and _____ really help in teamwork.

5 _____ is worse than _____.

6 In social situations, _____ is a terrible experience.

7 …

8 …

b 💬 Explain your ideas in 5a to a partner. Together decide on five key qualities and kinds of behavior that are important to social relationships.

c 💬 Choose one of the social situations below. What further problems might you have? How could you deal with them? Make a list of problems and suggestions.

* You have to live in an unfamiliar country for six months. You don't speak the language, and very few people speak English / your native language.
* You join a class and find that everybody there already knows each other.
* You are doing an online course. During your classes, you sense that your teacher is not paying attention.
* You meet someone you think is very interesting online, and you'd like to get to know them better.

d 💬 Have you / Has anyone you know ever been in any of the situations in 5c? How did you/they deal with it?

Learn to apologize and admit fault
- **S** Deal with a situation where you are at fault
- **P** Sound and spelling: *ou* and *ough*

1 LISTENING

a 💬🔊 Look at pictures a–d and answer the questions.

1 Why do you think each character is saying sorry?
2 Do you use the same word for all the situations in your language?

b ▶ 07.20 Seth is meeting his coworker Mike to discuss a project at work. Listen to Part 1. What is Seth apologizing for?

c ▶ 07.20 Listen to Part 1 again and answer the questions.

1 What is Mike's attitude toward the robot project?
2 How does Mike react to Seth's suggestion?
3 How does Seth feel at the end of the conversation?

d 💬🔊 Do you think Mike's reaction is justified?

2 PRONUNCIATION Sound and spelling: *ou* and *ough*

a ▶ 07.21 Listen to the sentences from Part 1. Write down one word spelled with *ou* in each sentence. What do you notice about the sounds of the letters in the words?

b ▶ 07.22 Match the words in the box to the correct sounds in the chart below. Which sounds are short and which are long? Listen and check.

| pron**ou**ncing sh**ou**ld consci**ou**s t**ou**gh en**ou**gh |
| th**ou**ght thr**ou**gh thor**ou**ghly c**ou**gh r**ou**gh |
| **ou**ght p**ou**r s**ou**th s**ou**thern r**ou**te |

1 /ʊ/	2 /u/	3 /aʊ/
could	soup	noun

4 /oʊ/	5 /ʌ/	6 /ɔ/
fourth	touch	

7 /ə/
jealous

c ▶ 07.23 Listen to the conversation. Then practice it in pairs. Pay attention to the words spelled with *ough*.

A I give up. I know it was supposed to be tough, but enough's enough.

B Have you thought it through thoroughly, though?

A Yes. I feel awful and I've got a terrible cough.

B Fair enough. You do look rough. You ought to take it easy.

3 LISTENING

a ▶ 07.24 Mike tells his sister Imani about his earlier meeting with Seth. Put events a–g in the order you think they will happen. Listen to Part 2 and check.

a ☐ Imani asks Mike about his meeting with Seth.
b ☐ 1 Imani shows Mike a diet on a website.
c ☐ Imani tries to boost Mike's confidence.
d ☐ Imani tells Mike off.
e ☐☐ Mike calms down.
f ☐ Mike decides to call Seth.
g ☐☐ Mike loses his temper.

b ▶ 07.24 Listen to Part 2 again. Do Imani and Mike agree that … ?

1 Mike should eat more healthfully
2 Adam's idea is good
3 Mike should apologize to Seth

c **Language in context** *Challenging*
Paraphrase the two sentences Mike says below.

1 Why don't you just come out with it?
2 Why doesn't everyone just get off my back?!

d 💬 What do you think of how Imani dealt with Mike's … ?

● angry outburst
● fears

How do you think Mike feels at the end of his conversation with Imani?

4 USEFUL LANGUAGE
Apologizing and admitting fault

a 💬 Look at the picture. What two things does the navigation system do when it speaks to the driver?

I do apologize. It was my fault entirely.

b ▶ 07.25 Complete the excerpts from Parts 1 and 2 with the words in the box. Listen and check.

line   thought   guess   inexcusable   came   right

1 It was _____ of me …
2 I was out of _____ / order.
3 I _____ I was helping. Sorry.
4 I don't know what _____ over me.
5 I had no _____ to take it out on you …
6 I _____ I overreacted …

c Which expression(s) in 4b could you use if … ?

a you had done something you wouldn't usually do
b you had been angry because you had a bad day
c you had said something that accidentally hurt somebody's feelings
d you had been more angry than you should have been about something small.

d 💬 Work in pairs. Plan the telephone conversation between Mike and Seth. Use the expressions in 4b. Role-play your conversation for the class.

Hi Seth, it's Mike.

Hi Mike. What can I do for you?

I'm calling to apologize for earlier. I was completely out of line …

5 SPEAKING

≫ **Communication 7C** Work in pairs. Student A: Go to p. 137. Student B: Go to p. 135.

✓ UNIT PROGRESS TEST

→ **CHECK YOUR PROGRESS**

YOU CAN NOW DO THE UNIT PROGRESS TEST.

Learn to write a proposal

W Proposals; Linking: highlighting and giving examples

1 LISTENING AND SPEAKING

a 💬 Look at photos 1–4 of people working in teams. What kinds of teams are they? Which photo represents your idea of teamwork?

b 💬 Answer the questions.

1 What teams have you been a part of?
2 Which of the teams worked well together? Which didn't?
3 What kinds of issues arose? Why? Think about:
   • productivity/achievements   • disagreements
   • communication   • energy and enthusiasm.

c ▶07.26 Listen to a team that works for an insurance company and answer the questions about each speaker.

Pablo | Masha | Sam | Vicki (team leader)

• Pablo / Masha / Sam
   1 Which coworker does the speaker focus on?
   2 What problem(s) does the speaker mention?
   3 What positive qualities do they mention?
• Vicki
   4 What's her opinion of the team? What does she plan to do?

d ▶07.26 Complete the summaries below with the words and phrases in the box. Listen again and check.

> attention to detail   cynical smile
> beneath him   annoys   unsettles   drawback
> caught up in their own agenda   lighten up
> goes off on tangents

1 Masha _____ Pablo when they have meetings.
2 Pablo thinks Masha should _____ and see the funny side of things.
3 Masha admires Sam's _____, but at the same time thinks it's sometimes a _____.
4 Pablo's silence _____ Sam, and he doesn't like the _____ on his face.
5 Sam often _____ in team meetings.
6 The expression on Pablo's face gives the impression that everything is _____.
7 Each team member is _____ and they all communicate poorly.

e 💬 Order these personality attributes 1–6 (1 = most tolerable; 6 = least tolerable).

☐ pays a lot of attention to detail
☐ has a cynical smile
☐ is insincere
☐ goes off on tangents
☐ thinks most others are beneath them
☐ is caught up in their own agenda

Compare with a partner. Give reasons for your order.

2 READING

a Read the proposal Vicki wrote for a team-building program for the consideration of senior management. Why has she chosen The Interpersonal Gym? How does she imagine the program will help her team?

b 💬 Imagine you are on Vicki's team. What would your reaction be when you hear about the team-building program?

3 WRITING SKILLS

Proposals; Linking: highlighting and giving examples

a Choose a word from the box to complete the headings in the proposal.

benefits   do   needs

b Underline the first person phrases in the proposal. Why does Vicki use these phrases? Check (✓) all the reasons.

- [ ] to introduce her opinions
- [ ] to sound more informal
- [ ] to be more persuasive

> 💬 **Writing Tip**
>
> It is always important to consider your audience and adjust the style of the language you use. Vicki's proposal is written for senior management, so a more formal style is appropriate. However, if she were writing to her team members, she would use a more relaxed style.

c Look at the highlighted words and phrases in the proposal. Which are used to … ?

1 give an example
2 give evidence
3 give more detailed information
4 highlight an individual thing, person, etc.

d Complete the paragraph below with the words in the box. Add the three words or phrases to the categories in 3c.

shown   such   especially

Group activities, [1]_____ problem-solving activities, are usually successful at building rapport among team members. An activity [2]_____ as finding the way out of a maze uses both cognitive and practical skills. A very dysfunctional team did this and bonded as a result. They now work together extremely well as [3]_____ by a 20% increase in their productivity.

e ≫ Now go to Writing Focus 7D on p. 173.

Introduction

The aim of this proposal is to outline plans to address training needs within my team.

Training _____

Recent team meetings have highlighted some breakdowns in communication in the team I currently manage. Specifically, the need for greater interpersonal awareness within a team framework has become apparent. I have identified one professional development day in particular that I believe is ideal.

The TIG program – what they _____

The Interpersonal Gym (TIG) has been running personal development programs for the past 12 years. As detailed in the attached brochure, TIG's specialty is team-building programs. These involve games and problem-solving activities that are likely to appeal to all team members. For instance, there are simple but effective trust-building exercises in which team members have to help a partner negotiate a series of obstacles when blindfolded. The training places an emphasis on strategies to enhance active listening and collective decision-making.

_____ to our business

I believe the TIG program will offer effective professional development. TIG has an excellent reputation, as demonstrated by their impressive range of testimonials from organizations similar to our own. Overall, the program is likely to have a number of benefits for the business, namely increased sales and job satisfaction among team members, and therefore lower absenteeism and increased profits.

Conclusion

I hope you will agree that a training session run by TIG would be a practical and worthwhile way of addressing issues that are affecting the team's productivity.

4 WRITING

a 💬 Choose one of the teams below and imagine you are its program leader. What kind of training or team-building activities do you think would help?

1 an admin team that has absenteeism problems
2 a sales team that isn't selling very much
3 a student council that cannot agree on anything
4 a sports team lacking in motivation to do better

b ≫ **Communication 7D** Now go to p. 137 and choose a team-building program for your team.

c Write a proposal to someone in authority for a team-building personal development day.

- Indicate which day you plan to go on and why.
- Describe how you think the team building will benefit the team.
- Remember to be gently persuasive and use formal language.

d 💬 Imagine you are the person in authority. Read another student's proposal. Will you accept it? Why / Why not?

1 GRAMMAR

a Choose the correct option.

1 I'm sure the new version *may / will / should* work well.
2 I *couldn't / wouldn't / must not* have gone out last night; I was exhausted.
3 It's highly unlikely *for flying cars to / that flying cars will* appear.
4 There *may / can / must* be no such thing as paper money in 50 years.
5 Sorry, you did tell me. I *may / can / must* have forgotten.
6 This will be a good opportunity, and it *must / should / has got to* take you places.

b Complete the sentences with the words in the box.

not	happened	was	only	did	what	all	it

1 _____ interests me most is how stress affects relationships.
2 It was my youngest daughter who _____ the most affected.
3 What _____ was that Simon started spending less time at home.
4 _____ is Sue who needs to rethink her priorities, not me.
5 _____ that I am asking for is a little commitment.
6 It was _____ until the following day that Richard told his wife.
7 What I _____ was rearrange the seating plan.
8 It was _____ when I left home that I appreciated my parents.

2 VOCABULARY

a Correct the mistakes in the compound adjectives.

1 Sue is so hot-hearted that she'd do anything for anybody.
2 Cutting wood all day was really spine-breaking work.
3 Write it down for me because I'm getting rather absence-minded.
4 It's mind-wobbling what you can do with technology today.
5 The comedy is a light-headed look at what really goes on in hospitals.
6 To leave after all those years was heart-cracking.

b Replace the words in *italics* with the noun form of a word in the box.

collaborate	innovate	liberate	nervous
optimistic	rude	selfish	

1 There was great *anxiety* among the crowd as they waited to find out the result.
2 What will be the next *new thing* in cell phone technology?
3 There is no excuse for *being impolite*.
4 We are proud to announce our *teamwork* on this project.
5 You can look to the future with some *positive feelings*.
6 *Only thinking about yourself* is common in society today.
7 The *freeing* of Paris in 1945 was an important event.

3 WORDPOWER *self-*

a ▶07.27 Replace the words in *italics* with the adjectives in the box. Listen and check.

self-sacrificing	self-centered	self-aware
self-confident	self-sufficient	self-satisfied

1 I'm sure she'll be a successful team leader. She's very *certain of her own abilities*.
2 Yoga is good for your health, and it also makes you more *able to notice your thoughts and feelings*.
3 He doesn't care about anyone else. I've never met anyone who's so *interested only in his own needs*.
4 She's so *pleased with herself* that it never occurs to her that other people don't like her.
5 She gave up her job so her husband could pursue a career in politics. Why is she always so *ready to give up things for other people*?
6 We've started growing our own vegetables, although I doubt we'll ever be *able to look after our own needs*.

b Complete the text with adjectives from 3a.

I have always thought of myself as a pretty successful person. I'm [1]_____ – for example, I don't get nervous if I have to give a presentation at work. I'm also [2]_____ – I earn enough money to pay my bills and buy the things I want to. But then I went with a friend to a self-help course, and I realized that maybe I was wrong to be so pleased with myself. I was so concerned with my own life that I hadn't stopped to think about anyone else's. Maybe I was actually just [3]_____? What if other people saw me as being just too pleased with myself – [4]_____, even! This was such a horrible thought, I immediately decided to be more [5]_____ and give up some of my time to help other people, and now I volunteer at a homeless shelter. This does make me feel good about myself, though, so maybe I haven't really changed at all? Well, at least I've started thinking about this, so hopefully I've become a little more [6]_____.

c 💬 Use adjectives from 3a to describe:
- yourself
- people you know
- well-known people.

Discuss your ideas with a partner.

⟳ REVIEW YOUR PROGRESS

How well did you do in this unit? Write 3, 2, or 1 for each objective.

3 = very well   2 = well   1 = not so well

I CAN ...	
speculate about inventions and technology	☐
emphasize opinions about the digital age	☐
apologize and admit fault	☐
write a proposal.	☐

CAN DO OBJECTIVES

- Describe sleeping habits and routines
- Talk about lifestyles and life expectancy
- Negotiate the price of a product or service
- Write promotional material

BODY AND HEALTH

UNIT **8**

GETTING STARTED

a 💬 Look at the picture and answer the questions.

1 How old do you think the woman in the photo is?
2 Why do you think the woman's decided to do this activity? Is it the first time? Will it be the last?
3 What do you think the relationship between her and the other people in the picture is?
4 What other activities might this woman and her peers enjoy? Make a list.

b 💬 Do you think it's more or less important to do physical activity as you get older? Why?

91

8A | THERE'S NO USE TRYING TO GO TO SLEEP

Learn to describe sleeping habits and routines
G Gerunds and infinitives
V Sleep

1 SPEAKING AND READING

a 💬 Do you know the answers to these questions? If not, what do you think they are?

1 Why do all animals (including humans) need sleep?
2 What percentage of their life does the average person spend asleep?
3 How long is it possible to go without sleep?
4 How many hours a night should adults sleep? What about newborn babies?

b ▶ 08.01 Listen to the radio interview and check your answers.

c 💬 Look at these headings for four tips for people who have problems getting to sleep. What do you think each tip involves?

> Acknowledge distractions   Everybody out!
> It is what it is   Compile a playlist

Read the article and match the headings with tips A–D.

d 💬 Do you think the tips would work for you?

2 GRAMMAR Gerunds and infinitives

a Look at the highlighted phrases in the article. Which phrases are followed by … ?

a an infinitive: *1 too much*
b a base form:
c gerund (verb + *-ing*):

b Look at examples 1–4. Match the verb forms in **bold** with a–d.

1 Enjoy **being soothed** to sleep by music.
2 It's easy **to be distracted** by background noises.
3 Go to work tomorrow without **having had** eight hours' sleep.
4 Be pleasantly surprised **to have slept** all night long.

a ☐ passive infinitive   c ☐ passive gerund
b ☐ perfect infinitive   d ☐ perfect gerund

c Look at these examples. What, if anything, is the difference in meaning between each pair?

1 a He got out of bed without saying a word.
   b He got out of bed without having said a word.
2 a He seems to sleep well.
   b He seems to have slept well.
3 a My daughter likes reading in bed.
   b My daughter likes being read to in bed.
4 a I'd like to wake up at 8:30.
   b I'd like to be woken up at 8:30.

TOP TIPS to Help You Sleep

Do you lie awake at night counting sheep? After a long day at work or college, do you find there's [1]too much to think about and your head is spinning?

Trying to get to sleep can be very frustrating. You might lie awake for hours until it gets to about [2]five or six o'clock in the morning and then decide [2]there's no use trying to go to sleep and you [3]may as well get up. Here are four tips to help you get to sleep quickly:

A _____

If you enjoy being soothed to sleep by music, why not create the ultimate collection of soothing tracks? Choose songs with few or no lyrics and avoid anything with a catchy tune. When [4]it's time to sleep, turn the volume down as low as possible.

B _____

When you're trying to fall asleep, it's very easy to become irritated by background noises. However, sometimes [5]the best way to deal with them is by accepting them. Say to yourself, "I can hear the clock, but it doesn't bother me," or "I like the neighbor's music." Soon they'll become less important.

C _____

Imagine your body is full of tiny people all working away with hammers. Announce that their shift is over so they[6]'d better go home. Imagine them all putting their tools down and leaving your body one by one through your feet. This will make you relax, and you should soon drift off to sleep.

D _____

[7]There's no point in making judgments ("I should have been asleep hours ago") or indulging in catastrophic thinking ("If I go to work tomorrow without having had eight hours' sleep, I'll mess up that presentation, lose my job, and die tired and alone"). Make the night easier by accepting it for what it is, letting go of judgments, and being gentle with yourself. The silver lining? You just might get to see a glorious sunrise.

So, for the chronic insomniacs out there, try some of these tips, and by the time you wake up in the morning, you may be pleasantly surprised to have slept all night long!

92

d Think of possible endings for these sentences. Then compare with other students.

1 I've got to get up at 4:00 to go to the airport, so I may as well …
2 If you don't feel tired, there's no point …
3 You can't keep sleeping only two hours a night. You'd better …
4 What a disaster! I went into the exam without having … (+ past participle)
5 When I feel tired, I really don't enjoy being … (+ past participle)
6 If you can't sleep, just accept it. There's no use …

e ≫ Now go to Grammar Focus 8A on p. 152.

3 READING

a Read the title of the article. What do you think the article will tell you about sleeping eight hours a night? Think of two possibilities. Read the article and check.

b Which of these are reasonable conclusions to draw from the article, and which aren't?

1 If there's nothing to interfere with them, most people would probably sleep in two segments.
2 In the 15th century, city streets probably would have been full of people at night.
3 The habit of sleeping for eight hours without waking up probably started in Europe.
4 People started going to bed later because the streets became less dangerous.
5 Stress in modern life is mainly a result of not sleeping well.

c Language in context *Cause, origin, and effect*

1 What do the highlighted words and phrases mean? Match the expressions with the definitions.

1 be a factor in, contribute to
2 be because of (x2)
3 spread to
4 take from
5 say that the cause was

2 Why do you think the writer preferred each highlighted expression?

d 💬 Do you agree that "lying awake could be good for you"? What arguments can you think of against Dr. Jacobs' point of view?

THE MYTH OF THE Eight-Hour SLEEP

We often worry about lying awake in the middle of the night – but it could be good for you. A growing body of evidence from both science and history suggests that the eight-hour sleep may be unnatural.

In the early 1990s, psychiatrist Thomas Wehr conducted an experiment in which a group of people were plunged into darkness for 14 hours every day for a month. It took some time for their sleep to regulate, but by the fourth week, the subjects had settled into a very distinct sleeping pattern. They slept first for four hours, then woke for one or two hours before falling into a second four-hour sleep. Though sleep scientists were impressed by the study, among the general public the idea that we must sleep for eight consecutive hours persisted.

In 2001, historian Roger Ekirch of Virginia Tech published a seminal paper, drawn from 16 years of research, revealing a wealth of historical evidence that humans used to sleep in two distinct chunks. His book *At Day's Close: Night in Times Past*, published four years later, unearths more than 500 references to a segmented sleeping pattern – in diaries, court records, medical books, and literature.

During the waking period between sleeps people were quite active. They often got up, went to the bathroom or smoked tobacco, and some even visited neighbors. Most people stayed in bed, read, wrote, and often prayed. Countless prayer manuals from the late 15th century offered special prayers for the hours in between sleeps.

Ekirch found that references to the first and second sleep started to disappear during the late 17th century. This started among the urban upper classes in northern Europe, and over the course of the next 200 years, filtered down to the rest of Western society. By the 1920s, the idea of a first and second sleep had receded entirely from our social consciousness. He attributes the initial shift to improvements in street lighting and domestic lighting and a surge in coffeehouses, which were sometimes open all night. As the night became a place for activity and as that activity increased, the length of time people could dedicate to rest dwindled.

Today, most people seem to have adapted quite well to the eight-hour sleep, but Ekirch believes many sleeping problems may have roots in the human body's natural preference for segmented sleep as well as the ubiquity of artificial light. This could be at the root of a condition called sleep maintenance insomnia, where people wake during the night and have trouble getting back to sleep, he suggests. The condition first appears in literature at the end of the 19th century, at the same time as accounts of segmented sleep disappear. "For most of evolution we slept a certain way," says sleep psychologist Dr. Gregg Jacobs. "Waking up during the night is part of normal human physiology."

Jacobs suggests that the waking period between sleeps, when people were forced into periods of rest and relaxation, could have played an important part in the human capacity to regulate stress naturally. In many historic accounts, Ekirch found that people used the time to meditate on their dreams. "Today we spend less time doing those things," says Dr. Jacobs. "It's not a coincidence that, in modern life, the number of people who report anxiety, stress, and depression has gone up." So the next time you wake up in the middle of the night, think of your pre-industrial ancestors and relax. Lying awake could be good for you.

4 LISTENING AND VOCABULARY Sleep

a 💬 You will hear four people talk about waking up at night. Look at the words below. What do you think each person is going to say?

ten or eleven – restless – photos – storm

1 Matt

yoga – studio – 20 other people – husband

2 Adriana

artist – image – dream – therapeutic

3 Bernie

village – friends – sunset – fire – sweet potato

4 Ignacio

b ▶ 08.04 Listen to the radio show. Were your ideas in 4a correct?

c Look at the expressions in the box from the recording. Which are about … ?

1 sleeping well or too long
2 not sleeping or not sleeping well
3 falling asleep
4 having a short sleep

---

take a nap   be fast asleep   be wide awake
drift off to sleep   be a light sleeper   be restless
sleep like a log   not sleep a wink   toss and turn
oversleep   suffer from insomnia   doze off

---

d ▶ 08.05 **Pronunciation** Listen to this extract from the recording. Underline the stressed syllables in the fixed expressions in **bold**.

My wife used to force me to **get out of bed** 'cause I would lie there **tossing and turning** all night and I **couldn't sleep a wink**.

e ▶ 08.06 Underline the syllables you think will be stressed in the expressions in **bold**. Listen and check.

Sometimes I even get my husband to join us, if he's **having trouble sleeping**. But most of the time, **he's fast asleep** and doesn't even notice when I get up. He **sleeps like a log**!

f 💬 Talk about your sleeping habits using expressions from 4c. Use the questions below to help you plan what you are going to say.

1 Are they the same as people you live with? Why / Why not?
2 In what situations does your sleep pattern change? What can be different about it?
3 Do you know someone with particularly unusual sleeping habits?

5 SPEAKING

a 💬 Work in groups. Imagine that most people have segmented sleep patterns. What impact would it have on the way our lives are organized? How would society need to adapt? Consider these factors:

• travel and transportation   • entertainment and socializing
• work   • leisure activities   • education   • mealtimes.

b 💬 Plan a typical day for a student who wants to start a segmented sleep pattern. How can they make the best use of their time? When should they … ?

• eat   • work   • relax   • learn   • exercise
• spend time with friends

c 💬 Choose one student from your group to explain your idea to the class.

d 💬 Decide which group's plan is:

• the most practical   • the most original.

8B | SUPPOSE YOU COULD LIVE FOREVER

Learn to talk about lifestyles and life expectancy
G Conditionals
V Aging and health

1 SPEAKING AND VOCABULARY
Aging and health

a 💬 Look at the photos and read the quote. How do they make you feel?

> **Aging is one of the most profitable fears of our time.**

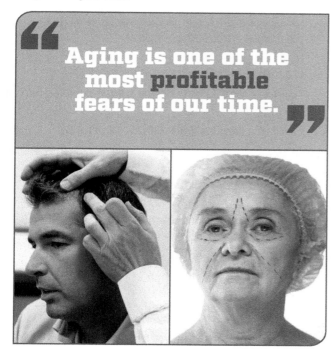

b 💬 Read about five treatments. Which do you think is the strangest? Which would you try?

c Match the highlighted words and phrases with the definitions.

1 _____ (adj.) of or on the face
2 _____ (adj.) clean and pleasant
3 _____ (n.) the movement of blood around the body
4 _____ (n.) lines on your face that you get when you grow old
5 _____ (n.) a temporary skin condition involving groups of small spots
6 _____ (n.) permanent marks left on the body from cuts or other injuries
7 _____ (adj.) not soft or loose, strong and healthy
8 _____ (n.) a beauty treatment involving gentle rubbing of creams into the face
9 _____ (n. phrase) the warm, healthy appearance of the skin on someone's face
10 _____ (n. phrase) the warm, healthy appearance of the skin typical of young people
11 _____ (adj.) hanging loosely, less tight than before

d ⟫ Now go to Vocabulary Focus 8B on p. 165.

Anti-Aging Treatments

Afraid of anti-aging injections?
Try these alternative treatments to make you look younger!

Snail Slime Cream
Carefully collected snail's slime is a potent anti-aging ingredient that helps reduce scars, acne, and skin rashes, as well as smoothing out wrinkles.

Emu Oil

Rendered from the fat of an emu bird, emu oil is a lesser known anti-aging oil that has been used for centuries in the Aboriginal communities for its healing powers. It leaves you with a glowing complexion.

Bee Sting Venom
The bee sting venom facial doesn't involve a swarm of bees stinging your face, but instead, the venom from the sting is transferred into a gel and then rubbed on the face as part of an intensive facial. It leaves your skin feeling fresh and renewed.

Anti-Sagging Lips

You can use a special rubbery mouthpiece to exercise your cheeks and lips. It is designed to keep the facial muscles firm by holding the cheeks and mouth stretched in a permanent "trout pout" position. It will help bring back smooth, healthy-looking cheeks.

"Platza" Treatment
The "platza" treatment involves the bare back being beaten with a "broom" made of oak-leaf branches. It was first used in the *banyas* (saunas) of Russia and in Turkish baths. This alternative massage is designed to stimulate the blood circulation, creating a youthful glow.

2 READING

a 💬 In the future, how likely do you think it is that medical science will keep people alive for much longer than today? Why do you think so?

b Read the interview with a scientist, Aubrey de Grey. How does he answer the question in 2a?

c Read the interview again. Summarize the main points made about these topics in paragraphs 2–7.

Paragraph 2: Diseases in old age
Paragraph 3: Attitudes toward the aging process
Paragraph 4: The challenge our body faces
Paragraph 5: Aubrey de Grey and the medical profession
Paragraph 6: People who might benefit
Paragraph 7: Managing the population

d 💬 Would you like to live for 1,000 years? Why / Why not?

We don't have to **get sick** as we get **older**

by Caspar Llewellyn Smith

Aubrey de Grey, expert in gerontology and Chief Science Officer, *SENS Research Foundation*

1 With his beard and robust opinions, there's something of the philosopher about Aubrey de Grey. De Grey studied computer science at Cambridge University but became interested in the problem of aging more than a decade ago.

2 What's so wrong with getting old?

It is simply that people get sick when they get older. I don't often meet people who want to suffer cardiovascular disease or whatever, and we get those things as a result of the lifelong accumulation of various types of molecular and cellular damage. This is harmless at low levels, but eventually it causes the diseases and disabilities of old age – which most people don't think are any fun.

3 Why does the world not recognize the problem of aging?

People have been trying to claim that we can defeat aging since the dawn of time, and they haven't been terribly successful; there is a tendency to think there is some sort of inevitability about aging – it somehow transcends our technological abilities in principle, which is complete nonsense.

3 GRAMMAR Conditionals

a Read the web comments about longevity. Which ones reflect your opinion?

(1) I would be a little more relaxed about my life goals if it were actually possible to live for a thousand years!

(2) If medical science had been more advanced a hundred years ago, the world population would be out of control today.

(3) Assuming what Aubrey de Grey says is correct, we probably don't need to worry so much about exercise and diet.

(4) Supposing that we all were able to live for a very long time, people would just stop having children.

(5) Had I been born 200 years ago, I would have been astounded to be told about life expectancies in the year 2000.

(6) I won't care about living to a ripe old age as long as I feel I've had an interesting life.

(7) Even if I only lived to a hundred, that'd be an amazing achievement.

REPLY 📧

b Which sentences in 3a refer to … ?

a a real possibility
b an imaginary or unreal situation
c both the past and the present

c Underline the word or phrase in each example in 3a that introduces the condition.

d ≫ Now go to Grammar Focus 8B on p. 153.

e 💬 Use the phrases in the box to talk about yourself. Say one thing that isn't true or you don't really believe. Can you guess which of your partner's statements isn't true?

Assuming that …   Had I …   Even if I only …
Supposing that …   If I hadn't …   As long as …

Talk about:
- living for a long time
- lifestyle and health
- life goals
- the future of the planet.

4 Is it that our bodies just stop being so proactive about living?

Basically, the body does have a vast amount of inbuilt anti-aging machinery; it's just not 100% comprehensive, so it allows a small number of different types of molecular and cellular damage to happen and accumulate. The body does try as hard as it can to fight these things, but it is a losing battle.

5 You say you want to enrich people's lives. Why is that?

The fact is, people don't want to get sick. I don't work on longevity; I work on keeping people healthy. The only difference between my work and the work of the whole medical profession is that I think we're within striking distance of keeping people so healthy that at 90 they'll carry on waking up in the same physical state as they were at the age of 30.

4 LISTENING

a 💬 Why do people follow special diets? Talk about different reasons. Have you (or has someone you know) ever had to follow a diet? How was it?

b 💬 Read about a calorie restricted (CR) diet. What kind of food do you think you can eat on this diet?

c ▶08.11 Listen to Peter Bowes talk to Martin Knight, who follows a CR diet. Answer the questions.

1 What does Martin do with the food in the photos below?
2 What does Martin's daily routine involve?

d ▶08.11 Listen again. Take notes on these topics.

1 eating out (discussed twice)
2 the look and taste of Martin's breakfast
3 Martin's lifestyle in general
4 Martin's reasons for following a CR diet
5 how Martin feels

e 💬 Do you think you could follow a CR diet? Why / Why not? If you did, what would the biggest sacrifice or challenge be in relation to your current lifestyle?

f ▶08.12 **Pronunciation** Listen to this extract.

1 Is the pitch lower or higher in the phrases in **bold**?

   Then I have sprouted oats, **16 grams**, so that's 70. Then this tomato paste here, **33 grams of that**, and almost done now. There we go. And then finally, I add some olive oil, **that's 9.2**.

2 Does this happen because the speaker repeats information or adds extra information?

g 💬 Describe the process of preparing a typical breakfast, lunch, or dinner to a partner. Vary your pitch as in the example above. Can you guess which meal your partner's describing?

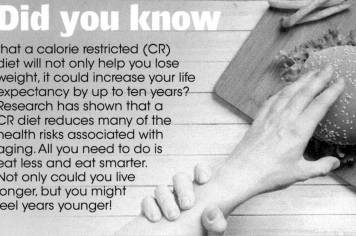

Did you know

that a calorie restricted (CR) diet will not only help you lose weight, it could increase your life expectancy by up to ten years? Research has shown that a CR diet reduces many of the health risks associated with aging. All you need to do is eat less and eat smarter. Not only could you live longer, but you might feel years younger!

5 SPEAKING

a 💬 When have you or someone you know been told you were too young or too old to do something? Explain what happened.

b 💬 Work in small groups. What are your opinions of these statements? Talk about your own experiences.

> 1 How old someone feels depends entirely on their health.
> 2 TV ads in my country represent older people in realistic ways.
> 3 It's easier for people under forty to get a job than those over forty.
> 4 The longer you live, the more eccentric you become.
> 5 Companies that sell anti-aging products don't want people to feel good about themselves.

c 💬 For each of the statements, choose one person in your group to tell the class their opinion and describe their experience. Take a class vote on who agrees and disagrees with each statement.

6 You've said you think the first person to live to 1,000 may already be alive. Could that person be you?

It's conceivable that people in my age bracket, their 40s, are young enough to benefit from these therapies. I'd give it a 30% or 40% chance. But that is not why I do this – I do this because I'm interested in saving 100,000 lives a day.

7 Can the planet cope with people living so long?

That's to do with the balance of birth and death rates. It didn't take us too long to lower the birth rate after we more or less eliminated infant mortality 100 or 150 years ago. I don't see that it's sensible to regard the risk of a population spike as a reason not to give people the best healthcare that we can.

chard

sprouted oats

kale

1 LISTENING

a 💬🔊 Answer the questions.

1 What was the most memorable present you received as a child?
2 Who was it from?
3 Have you ever sold anything that was valuable to you?

b 💬🔊 You are going to hear Tatyana talking about a present she received as a child. What kinds of presents often have sentimental value?

c ▶️ 08.13 Listen to Part 1. Does Tatyana mention one of your ideas in 1b? Who made this present? What does she want to do with it?

d 💬🔊 What do you think Tatyana will do next?

e ▶️ 08.14 Listen to Part 2 and answer the questions.

1 Why does Tatyana meet with Miranda?
  a to find out the value of her watch
  b to find out what she knows about rare watches
  c to trade watches
  d to talk about her grandfather
2 How would you describe the relationship between Tatyana and Miranda?
  a friendly
  b familiar
  c businesslike
  d hostile
3 Who do you think is the better negotiator?
  a Tatyana
  b Miranda

f ▶️ 08.14 Listen to Part 2 again. Then write a possible *Why* question for each answer.

1 So that Miranda will understand that the watch is one of a kind.
2 So that Miranda will believe her information is from a reliable source.
3 Because she hasn't authenticated what Tatyana is offering yet.
4 Because she's concerned she won't be able to authenticate the watch.

g **Language in context** *Expressions with* fair
Match expressions 1–3 with meanings a–c.

1 ☐ it's fair to say
2 ☐ fair's fair
3 ☐ fair enough

a this is reasonable
b I understand this
c this is true

h 💬🔊 Answer the questions.

1 Do you think Tatyana is behaving fairly? What about Miranda?
2 How do you think these people would react if they knew what Tatyana had done?
  • her grandfather • her mother • Helen

2 USEFUL LANGUAGE Negotiating

a ▶ 08.15 Complete Tatyana and Miranda's conversation. Listen and check.

M Then **there's just the** ¹_____ **of** how much you would like for it.

T Well, **how much would you be** ²_____ **to pay**?

M I think **we'd be** ³_____ **to offer**, say, two fifty? **Would that be a** ⁴_____ **suggestion**?

T Two fifty! **How about we** ⁵_____ that a little? **I was kind of** ⁶_____ **for something more in the region of** five hundred.

M No, that would be ⁷_____ **of the question. What would you** ⁸_____ **to** three fifty? In principle, of course. I'd need to complete the authentication first.

T Three fifty – **is that your** ⁹_____ **offer**?

b Add the expressions in **bold** in 2a to the correct category.

Opening negotiations	Making and accepting offers
I'm open to suggestions/discussion.	I'd be authorized/prepared to accept … I'm not in a position to offer more than …

Asking for more	Declining offers
It's worth much more than that. How flexible can you be on that?	I'm not authorized to accept anything less.

c 💬 Complete the conversation with words from the chart. Practice it with a partner.

A How much would you like for it?

B I'm ¹_____ to suggestions.

A I think we could go to five.

B It's ²_____ much more than that. I'd be prepared to ³_____ seven.

A How ⁴_____ can you be on that? I'm not in a ⁵_____ to offer more than six.

B I'm not ⁶_____ to accept anything less than seven.

d 💬 Read the conversation below and answer the questions.

1 How is it the same as / different from the conversation in Part 2?

2 Which conversation would be more successful in real life? Why?

A How much do you want?	**A** No, 350.
B How much will you pay?	**B** No more?
A 250.	**A** No. I'll pay after 1:00.
B How about 500?	**B** Not now?
	A No.

3 PRONUNCIATION Sound and spelling: misleading vowels

a ▶ 08.16 Listen to these three words from the recording. They all have the spelling *ow*, but which one has a different sound?

how	know	now

b ▶ 08.17 Now listen to these groups of words that share vowel letters. You also heard them in the recording. Can you find the one word in each group that has a *different* vowel sound?

on	there	into	meant	of
one	were	in	heard	off
once	where	wind up	research	offer

c In the following words, what vowel sound do the letters in **bold** have? Work with a partner. Can you think of any other examples of these spellings with the same / different vowel sounds?

	Example: *(same spelling, same sound)*	Example: *(same spelling, different sound)*
h**o**ney	*m**o**ney*	*d**o**n't*
h**e**re		
k**i**nd		
ah**ea**d		
c**o**ffee		

4 SPEAKING

a Work alone. Think of an object or a service you could sell. Here are some ideas:

- an anti-aging treatment
- a new-generation smartphone
- a delivery service
- a car.

Make a list of selling points that might persuade someone to pay more for it.

b 💬 Work in pairs. Negotiate the price of your product or service. Use the language in 2a and 2b and implied questions.

✓ UNIT PROGRESS TEST

→ CHECK YOUR PROGRESS

YOU CAN NOW DO THE UNIT PROGRESS TEST.

8D SKILLS FOR WRITING
It's a unique dining experience

1 LISTENING AND SPEAKING

a 💬 Think about occasions when you eat out and answer the questions.

1 Do you think the food you eat out … ?
- usually tastes better than what you eat at home
- is usually healthier than what you eat at home
In what ways?

2 When you eat out, what things are most important to you? Choose the five most important things from this list.

- [ ] convenience
- [ ] presentation
- [ ] atmosphere
- [ ] health
- [ ] décor
- [ ] service
- [ ] value for money
- [ ] difference from food at home
- [ ] taste of the food
- [ ] quality of ingredients
- [ ] good reputation
- [ ] type of cuisine (e.g., vegetarian, Chinese)

b 💬 You are going to listen to a restaurant chef talking about a "Stone Age diet." What do you think this might mean?

c ▶ 08.18 Listen to the interview and answer the questions.

1 Why was the Paleolithic period significant in human development?
2 What foods does Julia believe are healthy, and why?
3 Why does Julia believe that dairy products and rice are unhealthy?
4 What are the similarities and differences between the food served at *Ancestors* restaurant and Paleolithic food?
5 To what extent do you agree with Julia's views about food and health?

d 💬 Do you agree with each of these statements about diets? Why / Why not?

1 People are always thinking of new diets. It's just a way to make money.
2 The best diet is to eat whatever you feel like eating because your body knows what it needs.
3 It's better to think about changing your eating habits for life than to go on a short-term diet.

2 READING

a 💬 Quickly read the home page of *Ancestors* restaurant and answer the questions.

1 What new information not mentioned by Julia do you find out on the home page?
2 What kind of customer would go to *Ancestors*, and why? Would you go there yourself?

b 💬 What else do you think is on the menu at *Ancestors*? Imagine one starter, one main dish, and one dessert. Then compare your answers.

ANCESTORS RESTAURANT

| Home | About | Menu | Location |

ANCESTORS RESTAURANT

Our city-center restaurant offers a unique dining experience. Lovingly prepared and exquisitely presented, our dishes contain only the purest ingredients, so you can be confident that our food is good for your body and your individual needs.
So many people eat healthy food at home but then bend the rules when it comes to eating out. At Ancestors, we have a different concept. We serve you the foods you can eat, not the foods you can't!

THE STONE AGE DIET

For thousands of years, we humans were hunter-gatherers: we thrived on meat, seafood, seasonal vegetables, grains, fruit, and nuts. Our bodies adapted to this diet, and it still suits our genetic makeup better than the recent additions of dairy products and processed foods. ***[Find out more …]***

At Ancestors, we believe that eating is all about two things: health and enjoyment. So we've created a Stone Age menu fit for 21st-century living.

③ WRITING SKILLS Promotional material; Using persuasive language

a Which of these do you think is the main purpose of the home page in 2a?

☐ to give detailed information   ☐ to give advice
☐ to promote the restaurant

b Why do you think the home page uses headings and short sections?

c Match the features of the home page 1–4 with their purposes a–d.

1 ☐ clear headings
2 ☐ short paragraphs
3 ☐ use of *we* and *you*
4 ☐ links

a to encourage the reader to browse the website
b to establish a personal relationship with the reader
c to show at a glance what the text is about
d to make it quick and easy to read

Healthy living	Opening times	Reservations

OUR MENU🌿

The menu at Ancestors changes according to the seasons. Signature dishes from head chef Julia Dean include sweet potato and hazelnut soup, lamb with sesame seeds, and smoked salmon with wild leaves. We also offer a range of desserts made to the most exacting standards, using only wild fruits and natural sweeteners. **[Sample menu ...]**

We take our drinks as seriously as our food. At Ancestors you'll find an exciting selection of natural fruit and vegetable juices from around the world, complemented by a range of teas, coffees, and herbal teas.

EARLY EVENING MENU🌿

Based in the city center, Ancestors is the ideal destination for a light and wholesome supper before you go to the theater or the movies. Tasty and fresh, the early evening menu offers a range of Ancestors dishes at a fixed price. Available 5:30 to 7:00 p.m.

THE ANCESTORS COOKBOOK🌿

So many of you have asked for our recipes that we've produced our own cookbook, using ingredients you can buy at any grocery store. Tried and tested by our team of cooks, our recipes will enable you to recreate the Ancestors experience in your own kitchen.
[View sample pages ...]

d At the top of the *Ancestors* home page, there is a slogan missing. Which of these do you think would work best? Why?

> EAT LIKE OUR ANCESTORS DID
>
> FOOD THAT'S GOOD FOR YOU
>
> PURE ENJOYMENT, PURE HEALTH
>
> ONLY THE BEST

e The home page aims to give a positive message about the restaurant. Match phrases 1–4 from the first two sections with the messages a–d they convey.

1 ☐ a unique dining experience
2 ☐ Lovingly prepared and exquisitely presented
3 ☐ At *Ancestors* we believe that
4 ☐ fit for 21st-century living

a The food is not at all old-fashioned.
b The food is made with care and looks good.
c *Ancestors* is not like other restaurants.
d What *Ancestors* is doing has a serious purpose.

f Compare these two sentences. Which emphasizes the positive features of the dishes more strongly? How is the structure different?

1 Lovingly prepared and exquisitely presented, our dishes contain only the purest ingredients.
2 Our dishes are lovingly prepared and exquisitely presented, and they contain only the purest ingredients.

Find three more examples of description at the front of a sentence in the text.

g ≫ Now go to Writing Focus 8D on p. 174.

④ WRITING

a 💬 Work in pairs or groups. Think of a concept for a restaurant. You could either invent one or base it on a place you know. Write down ideas for a promotional text on a website. Consider:

- the underlying concept
- how it's different from other places
- what it offers customers
- what its positive features are
- food and drink, décor, and atmosphere.

b Write a promotional text. Make sure you include clear headings, a name at the top, and an appealing slogan.

c 💬 Read other groups' texts and decide which restaurant you'd most like to visit. Think of additional questions and ask the other group about their restaurant.

1 GRAMMAR

a Choose the correct option.

1 *To wake / Waking / Having woken* up is easier in the summer.
2 *Being sent / Sending / Having sent* to boarding school is the best thing that ever happened to me.
3 I've always been a big fan of *to get / get / getting* up early.
4 Her refusal even *to listen / listening / for listening* to my idea really annoyed me.
5 There's no shame in *to have / having / being* lost to a team as good as theirs.
6 I was lucky enough *meeting / to have met / having met* Charles before he became famous.
7 Is there any hope *to save / of saving / saving* the lost sailors?

b Complete the sentences with one word.

1 I wouldn't be in such good shape if I _____ look after myself.
2 If Steve had said it one more time, I would _____ walked out.
3 _____ I known the photo meant so much to you, I would have kept it.
4 I'm going to say yes if Dave _____ me to marry him.
5 The trip needs to be well planned, _____ it will be a nightmare.
6 _____ we to find out that Emily wasn't lying, would you apologize?

2 VOCABULARY

a Match 1–8 with a–h.

1 ☐ It wasn't until about three that I finally
2 ☐ Mark is a light
3 ☐ I couldn't sleep a
4 ☐ We thought the baby was fast asleep, but she was wide
5 ☐ Don't worry, I sleep like
6 ☐ It can help to take
7 ☐ Gradually my eyes closed, and I started to drift
8 ☐ About 10% of adults suffer

a wink with all that building work going on.
b a little nap in the afternoon.
c dozed off.
d from insomnia of some kind.
e awake and getting restless.
f off to sleep.
g a log on trains.
h sleeper, so don't make too much noise.

b Which word is different from the others? Why?

1 smooth, saggy, clear, firm
2 scars, acne, a rash, blotches
3 tighten, moisturize, strengthen
4 tooth loss, hair loss, weight loss
5 whitening, yellowing, toning
6 wrinkles, poor circulation, hair loss

3 WORDPOWER *and*

a ▶08.19 Match sentences 1–6 with pictures a–f. Listen and check.

1 ☐ There are still just a few **odds and ends** to take away.
2 ☐ People came from **far and wide** to hear him talk.
3 ☐ It's **far and away** the best Italian restaurant in town.
4 ☐ I'm getting **sick and tired of** the noise.
5 ☐ It's just normal **wear and tear**.
6 ☐ It's just **part and parcel of** getting older, I suppose.

b Look at the phrases in **bold** in 3a. Replace each idiom with a non-idiomatic expression in the box.

easily   small things of different types
many places   annoyed by   a normal part of
damage caused by everyday use

c ▶08.20 Complete the sentences with the adjectives in the box. Listen and check.

tidy   safe   sweet   clear

1 "Can you hear me?"
   "Yes, I can hear you **loud and** _____."
2 "I'm almost afraid to touch anything in her room. She keeps it so **neat and** _____."
3 "I don't want to have a long discussion over the phone, so let's keep it **short and** _____."
4 "We got caught in a really bad blizzard, but fortunately we got home _____ **and sound**."

d Choose four expressions from 3a or 3c and write sentences but leave a blank for the expression.

e 💬 Read your sentences aloud. Can other students guess what goes in the blank?

↻ REVIEW YOUR PROGRESS

How well did you do in this unit? Write 3, 2, or 1 for each objective.
3 = very well   2 = well   1 = not so well

I CAN ...	
describe sleeping habits and routines	☐
talk about lifestyles and life expectancy	☐
negotiate the price of a product or service	☐
write promotional material.	☐

- Talk about city life and urban space
- Describe architecture and buildings
- Deal with conflict
- Write a discussion essay

UNIT 9

CITIES

GETTING STARTED

a 💬 Describe the buildings you can see in the picture.

b 💬 Answer the questions.
  1 Why do you think the building in the center of the picture hasn't been demolished?
  2 How do you think the following people feel about this house?
    - the owners
    - the local authorities
    - the other building's owners
    - other local residents

3 What do you think will happen to the house in the future? What will happen to the homeowner?

c 💬 If there were a plan to demolish your family home, under what circumstances would you agree?

103

Learn to talk about city life and urban space

G Reflexive and reciprocal pronouns
V Verbs with *re-*

The Day of the Pedestrian

In many cities around the world, mornings are a time of noise and traffic congestion: cars blow their horns as they maneuver around each other, buses grind their gears as they pull away from bus stops, and motorcycles rev their engines as they wait at traffic lights and crosswalks.

So imagine waking up in the center of a large city and hearing ... silence. No cars, no buses, no tires screeching or horns blaring. Only quieter, more soothing sounds: people chatting, children running and laughing, street vendors selling their wares, distant music, perhaps the sound of a bicycle bell.

This would be your experience on the morning of the "Day of the Pedestrian," which takes place annually in La Paz, Bolivia, on the first Sunday in September. The event, which is more properly titled the "Day of the Pedestrian and Cyclist in Defense of Mother Earth," is an expanded version of the *ciclovías* held in many cities across Latin America, where certain streets are closed to cars and dedicated to cyclists and pedestrians. Instead of closing just a few streets or a single main thoroughfare, however, all the roads in the capital city of La Paz and its neighboring city El Alto are closed for the whole day, from 8 a.m. to 6 p.m.

The immediate purpose of the event is to reclaim public streets for pedestrians and cyclists and reduce the consumption of fossil fuels. According to government statistics, carbon emissions are reduced by more than 60% on the day of the event. But its significance goes far beyond that: it also aims to increase public awareness of the negative effects of carbon emissions and air pollution by highlighting the contrast between the calm of the "Day of the Pedestrian" and the chaos of a normal day in La Paz.

Taking advantage of the sudden calm which has been restored to their city, locals stroll into the city center, pushing strollers, kicking soccer balls, and holding hands with their children. On El Prado, La Paz's main street, the periodic Sunday-morning fair is expanded, and the emphasis is on exercise and physical fitness. Organizers lay down turf for miniature soccer fields and volleyball courts. Aerobics classes are held in several locations, and skateboarders perform tricks in front of the crowds. In many streets, bands perform music and couples form pairs to dance the *Cueca Paceña*, a traditional Bolivian dance.

The "Day of the Pedestrian" is very popular among residents of the city, especially families who enjoy being able to allow their children out to play in the street without danger from traffic. Teachers are also strongly in favor of the initiative, since it offers an opportunity to provide environmental education about climate change and protecting the environment while at the same time focusing on exercise and enjoyment.

Even if only for one day a year, La Paz and El Alto are making a step toward a more traffic-free future, and the "Day of the Pedestrian" is an event to celebrate.

1 READING

a 💬🔊 Look at the photo of La Paz, the capital of Bolivia. Imagine yourself in the center of the city. What do you think it would be like? Think about:

streets	buildings	traffic
sounds	smells	people

b Read the first two paragraphs of the article. Is what you imagined more like the first paragraph, or more like the second?

c Read the rest of the article and answer the questions.
  1 What happens on the "Day of the Pedestrian"?
  2 What do people use the streets for?
  3 Is it generally popular among the residents of La Paz? Why / Why not?

d 💬🔊 Read the article again. What does it tell us about ... ?
  1 the difference between the "Day of the Pedestrian" and *ciclovías*
  2 carbon emissions in La Paz
  3 The Sunday morning fair on El Prado
  4 the *Cueca Paceña*
  5 El Alto
  6 the educational value of the "Day of the Pedestrian"

e 💬🔊 Imagine you live in La Paz. Would you take part in the "Day of the Pedestrian"? Why / Why not?

2 VOCABULARY Verbs with *re-*

a Look at the excerpts from the article. How are the words in bold similar in meaning?

The immediate purpose of the event is to **reclaim** public streets for pedestrians and cyclists.

Taking advantage of the sudden calm which has been **restored** to their city, locals stroll into the city center.

b ▶ 09.01 Complete the sentences with the correct forms of the verbs in the box that have the meaning shown in parentheses. Then listen and check.

recreate   redevelop   regain   regenerate
reinstate   rejuvenate   renovate

1 There are plans to _____ the port area of the city. (= improve it so that it becomes a more productive location to do business)
2 It's a beautiful old building. They just need to _____ it. (= repair and modernize it)
3 It's good that students are moving into the area. It will help to _____ it. (= give a younger and livelier atmosphere)
4 In order to make the movie, they _____ a Wild West town, complete with buildings and a railroad station. (= built a copy of it)
5 The town needs new industries so it will _____ its appeal as a place to live and work. (= get it back)
6 The city had decided to end the "Day of the Pedestrian," but after popular protests they agreed to _____ it. (= put it back again)
7 They are going to _____ the old airport and turn it into a shopping mall. (= change it by building new streets and buildings)

c ▶ 09.02 Pronunciation

1 Listen to the pronunciation of *e* in *re-* in the verbs in the chart.

1 /i/	2 /ɪ/
redevelop	rejuvenate

2 ▶ 09.03 Add the other verbs in 2a and 2b to the chart in question 1. Which verb has a different sound and can't be added to the chart? Listen and check.

d 💬 What buildings do you know of that have recently been renovated or restored? Are there parts of your city that need redeveloping or regenerating, in your opinion?

3 READING AND SPEAKING

a 💬 What do you think is happening in each photo A–D? Why do you think it was worth taking a photo of it?

b ≫ Communication 9A Work in groups of four: A, B, C, D. Student A: Go to p. 135. Student B: Go to p. 136. Student C: Go to p. 136. Student D: Go to p. 137.

c 💬 Explain the idea you read about to the other students. Which idea do you think … ?

- provides the most benefit to the community
- provides the least benefit
- would work best in your own city

4 GRAMMAR Reflexive and reciprocal pronouns

a Read the comments about the events in photos A–D. Which could they refer to?

1 It's a great place to just sit **by yourself**, drink coffee, and read the paper.
2 It just shows what local communities can do **for themselves**.
3 The place **itself** isn't very welcoming, but the people are.
4 People can sit and talk to **one another**.
5 It's a great neighborhood because we all support **each other**.
6 It's nice to have someplace people can make **themselves** comfortable while they wait for the bus.
7 Cars and pedestrians give way to **each other**. It really works.

b Look at the words and phrases in **bold** in 4a and answer the questions.

1 Which pronoun or phrase ending in *-self/-selves* … ?
   a ☐ shows that the object of the verb is the same as the subject
   b ☐ emphasizes one thing in contrast to something else
   c ☐ means *alone* or *not with other people*
   d ☐ means *independently, without help*
2 What is the difference between … ?
   a *we support ourselves* and *we support each other*
   b *they talk to themselves* and *they talk to one another*

c ≫ Now go to Grammar Focus 9A on p. 154.

5 LISTENING

a You are going to hear part of a podcast about how technology can improve life in cities. Look at the app in the picture. What do you think it is for?

b ▶ 09.06 Listen to the podcast and answer these questions.

1 How does the app work?
2 Why does Michelle think it's a good idea?
3 Do you agree with her? Would you use it? Why / Why not?

c ▶ 09.07 Listen to three more people talking about other ideas for "smart" cities. Two of them really exist and one is invented. Which do you think is the invented one? Why?

- Frank   • Rita   • Nick

d ▶ 09.07 Listen to each description again. Which idea (or ideas) … ?

1 gives live information
2 is useful for forgetful or absent-minded people
3 probably uses GPS
4 could be useful when it's raining
5 would be popular with hypochondriacs
6 could help you make friends

e In groups, talk about the ideas. Which idea … ?

- would you use yourself
- would you be prepared to pay for
- would other people you know use

f Answer the questions.

1 What other technology do you use or know of that makes city life easier?
2 To what extent do you think technology like that described makes people less self-reliant?

g Language in context *Colloquial expressions*

1 ▶ 09.08 Complete the expressions in **bold** below with the words in the box. Then listen and check.

keel	blow	place	whirl	neck
life	blend	dotted	smashed	

a … a place where you're repeatedly having to **risk your** _____ to get across the road.
b We're going past a park, and there's a railing that**'s been** _____ **in** here.
c So I can get the map here, _____ **it up** a bit like that.
d They have these screens all around the city; they're **all over the** _____.
e So let's **give it a** _____ … I put my finger on it.
f Let's see if I'm OK or whether I'm **about to** _____ **over**.
g These are artificial trees, and they're _____ **around** the city.
h They're shaped like trees, so they _____ **in**.
i I'm always going out without charging my phone, so it's **a real** _____**-saver** for me.

> **Learning Tip**
> A typical feature of colloquial English is the use of **phrasal verbs** rather than more formal, single-word verbs. When you come across a phrasal verb, notice if it has a single-verb equivalent and learn them both together.

2 Which phrasal verbs in 5g have the same meanings as *collapse* and *enlarge*?

6 SPEAKING

a Look at this list of ideas for making cities "smarter" or better to live in. Do any of them already exist in the city you live in or one you know? If so, how useful are they? If not, would you use the app or facility if it were available?

1 an app giving information about new projects and impending legislation in the city
2 parking apps to show drivers the nearest available parking space and how much it costs
3 apps to let users "adopt" city property, such as trash cans, trees, and flower beds, and volunteer to maintain them
4 digital parking payment systems, allowing you to pay for parking by smartphone, without using coins or tickets
5 free Wi-Fi everywhere in the city, including on trains, buses, and the subway
6 screens in public places that display traffic information, weather, and local news

b Work in groups of three. Choose an idea in 6a or your own idea that does not exist where you live yet and prepare to sell your idea to the class. Write notes of some things you could say about it:

- how it would work
- what benefit it would bring to the city
- possible problems and solutions.

c Give a group presentation. Focus on one point in 6b each. Vote on the best idea in the class.

9B | THEY WANTED A DRAMATIC SKYLINE AND THEY GOT ONE

Casa Batlló
Krzywy Domek (The Crooked House)
Triumph Palace
Torre Velasca
Museo Soumaya
The United Nations Secretariat Building

1 SPEAKING AND VOCABULARY
Describing buildings

a 💬 Have you seen these buildings before? What city and country do you think each is located in? What do you think they were built as? What do you think of each building?

b Which of the words and phrases in the box are positive? Which are negative? Check new words in a dictionary.

1 imposing	4 innovative	7 dated
2 nondescript	5 tasteless	8 out of place
3 graceful	6 over the top	9 stunning

c ▶09.09 **Pronunciation** Listen and <u>underline</u> the stressed syllable in each word or phrase in 1b.

d 💬 Use the words and phrases in 1b or other adjectives to describe the buildings in the pictures.

> The UN Building is fairly imposing, but it's a little nondescript.

> The Museo Soumaya is very graceful, but it's a little over the top.

e ⟫ Now go to Vocabulary Focus 9B on p. 166.

f 💬 Take turns describing local or iconic buildings that you think your partner will know about. Guess the building your partner is describing.

> It's an imposing building near the river. It used to be a warehouse.

> Is it the … ?

2 GRAMMAR Ellipsis and substitution

a 💬 Read sentences 1–6. Which of them are true for you or the place you live?

1 Most people dislike modern architecture. I know I **do**.
2 They don't consult residents about new buildings as often as they ought to ^.
3 They've put up that skyscraper and ^ ruined the skyline.
4 The old buildings are always being knocked down to make way for new **ones**.
5 The government promised they were going to build more houses, but they haven't ^ yet.
6 They haven't built anything new around here for a long time. **Nor** are they likely to.

b Look at each sentence in 2a again. Which words have been omitted (^) or substituted with words in **bold**? Why?

c ⟫ Now go to Grammar Focus 9B on p. 155.

3 READING

Jeanne Gang

a Read the article about the architect Jeanne Gang. Choose the best summary.

1 Jeanne Gang is an architect with a wide vision who is interested not only in the buildings she designs, but also the environments in which they are situated.

2 Jeanne Gang has become a world-famous architect because she has studied and traveled widely. She has integrated ideas she picks up on her travels into her designs, and as a result, has revolutionized the Chicago cityscape.

b Read the text again. Write notes on Jeanne Gang's:

- background and personality
- architectural style and a key building she designed
- environmental awareness
- interest in social justice
- core work philosophy.

c 💬 Talk about these questions.

1 Look at the photos of Jeanne Gang's buildings. What do/don't you like about the buildings?

2 To what extent does the environment in which a building is situated play a part in its success? Think of examples in your country where the environment has had a positive or negative impact on a building.

3 In what different ways can architects and builders help the environment?

d Language in context *Metaphorical phrases*

1 Notice how forms of the words in **bold** in the phrases below are used in the text. Is the meaning exactly the same?

a **walk** down the street
b a **blossoming** tree
c a **game** of tennis
d **sparks** from a fire
e heating **fueled** by gas
f the **hallmark** on a gold bracelet

2 Match the highlighted expressions in the article with the definitions.

a doing her best work
b created her initial motivation
c are examples of typical features
d won a prize or award
e a key event that causes a positive result
f develop and become more successful
g strongly increased her enthusiasm

> 💬 **Learning Tip** Many expressions include an indirect or metaphorical meaning. It can sometimes help to think about the literal meaning of key words as a way of understanding the expression. For example, a tree that blossoms suggests fresh and attractive new growth that will develop further.

She is the architect of the tallest building in the world designed by a woman. She has walked away with top architectural awards and commissions. From her local roots and early projects in Chicago, she has blossomed into one of the world's most celebrated and sought-after architects. *Time* magazine named her as one of the world's most influential people in 2019.

There's no doubt that Jeanne Gang is at the top of her game. Despite this, she is known to be genuine, open and easy to talk to with a classic Midwestern warmth and charm. While having offices around the world, she is very much a Chicago architect who has engaged with her city and its challenges. She is passionate about environmental and social concerns and the role that buildings play in the natural world.

Jeanne Gang grew up in a small town near Chicago. Her father was an engineer who took his family on trips that involved stopping to look at bridges. This clearly sparked Jeanne's interest in architecture as a child which then became evident when she started making buildings from ice and mud. She studied architecture at the University of Illinois and Harvard Graduate School of Design, and urban design as a visiting scholar at the Swiss Federal Institute of Technology in Zurich. This gave her an understanding not only of building construction but also engineering, landscape design and urban planning. This doubtless fueled her strong interest in the relationship between building and the environment.

After a period working in the Netherlands, Jeanne returned to Chicago and set up her own office, Studio Gang, in 1997. Since the beginning her work has included a great range of projects that show all the hallmarks of a typical Gang design: innovative elegance coupled with creative flare. The game-changer was the invitation to design Aqua Tower in Chicago which was completed in 2010. This 82-story building has been a spectacular success and even the most critical architects agree that it immediately became an architectural icon. What makes Aqua Tower distinctive are the irregular shaped balconies that give the impression of rippling water. Not only are they beautiful but they also are designed to give residents great views of the city, shield the windows from the sun and diminish the impact of Chicago's very strong winds on the building. The specific nature of Aqua Tower's design is as much a testament to Jeanne's understanding of engineering as it is to her architectural creativity.

Aqua Tower includes one of Chicago's largest green roofs, which is located atop its three-story base. This points to one of Jeanne's key concerns as an architect: environmentalism. When designing a building she always asks herself where

City Hyde Park, Chicago

4 LISTENING

a Look at the photo of the thin skyscrapers being built in New York. Why do you think people might like them or criticize them?

b ▶09.17 Listen to Maria and Ethan talk about thin skyscrapers. Who is for and against them? Who mentions the following points, Maria (M) or Ethan (E)?

1. ☐ spoiling the way New York looks
2. ☐ the way New York keeps changing
3. ☐ apartments that are unoccupied
4. ☐ Midtown's need for life
5. ☐ the extreme height of the buildings
6. ☐ affordable homes outside the city center
7. ☐ problems maintaining a building

c ▶09.17 Listen again and answer the questions.

1. What are "air rights"?
2. Why does Maria refer to the Empire State Building?
3. What does Ethan suggest by using the term *selling out*?
4. What is NIMBYism and what do you think are the consequences?

d 💬 What examples do you know of where there has been a controversy over urban development?

the resources to build it come from and what effect this will have on the environment. If there is any possibility of reusing or recycling material, that will always be her first choice. Her firm has undertaken a number of projects that focus on specific environmental issues. For example, the conversion of a coal-burning power plant into a modern student union building called the Beloit College Powerhouse in Wisconsin. Two public boathouses on the Chicago River designed by Studio Gang are playing a key role in reclaiming and cleaning up what was once a dirty and polluted waterway.

Jeanne is also broadening her focus to social justice issues. We often underestimate the degree to which buildings and urban design play a part in socioeconomic divisions within a city. Studio Gang has worked with police and community members in Chicago to come up with the concept of a 'Polis Station'. This involves envisioning how police stations can be redesigned to function more like community centers, where residents and police can find many opportunities to interact in non-enforcement situations. Another project in New York City is investigating how to improve safety and well-being in neighborhoods by creating pleasant civic spaces that allows citizens to interact freely. All of these social development projects are carried out in consultation with residents and community-based organizations as well as experts in areas like crime prevention and mental health.

Some say Jeanne runs the risk of spreading her focus too broadly. But she sees working on a great variety of projects as a way of ensuring her firm engages with a range of scales and materials. This informs the practice and makes their work more interesting. She also believes that irrespective of the size or purpose of a project, there are driving questions and conceptual ideas that connect all of the work and give it relevance for the wider world.

5 SPEAKING

a 💬 Read the scenario, talk about your ideas, and come up with a proposal and a reason for it.

There is a derelict warehouse in your community that was built in the early 20th century. You are a member of the city council, and you have to help make a decision about how the warehouse or the land itself could be repurposed.

Consider:

- the needs of your community
- demolition and rebuilding
- the benefits of a new, iconic building
- a high-profile architect
- your community's architectural heritage
- the warehouse's architectural features.

b 💬 Work in groups of four. Present your proposals to each other. Agree on one proposal and tell the class.

Aqua Tower, Chicago

9C EVERYDAY ENGLISH
Let's not jump to conclusions

Learn to deal with conflict
- S Complain and respond to complaints
- P Sound and spelling: foreign words in English

1 LISTENING

a 💬🔊 How would you feel if, without your permission, ... ?
- you saw yourself in a documentary about learning English
- your photo appeared on Google Earth
- a radio station called you live on air to offer you the chance to win a prize

b ▶09.18 Friends Jack and Victor are talking about Victor's recent success as a professional photographer. Look at the photo and listen to Part 1. Answer the questions.
1 What is on the screen?
2 Why is Victor angry about it?
3 What does he intend to do about it?

c ▶09.18 Read these phrases from Part 1. Who or what do the words in **bold** refer to? Listen to Part 1 again and check.
1 It seems like **everything's** falling into place.
2 Wow, **that's** awesome.
3 Who's going to shoot them? **This guy**.
4 **This** is outrageous!
5 Maybe **he** took the memory card!
6 I'm calling **them** right now.

d Language in context *Animal idioms*
1 ▶09.19 Correct the idioms from Part 1. Listen and check.
   a There's something horsey about this.
   b I smell an owl.
   c Hold your fish, Victor.

2 What do you think the idioms mean? Look at a dictionary if necessary.

e ▶09.20 Victor calls the editor-in-chief at *Free Voice Online* to complain. Listen to Part 2 and answer the questions.
1 How does Aaron respond to Victor's complaint? Does he ... ?
   a pass on the blame to someone else
   b accept responsibility and apologize
   c promise to take action and try to arrange a meeting
2 How do you think Victor feels after the phone call?
3 What do you think Aaron will do next?

2 USEFUL LANGUAGE
Dealing with conflict

a ▶09.18 ▶09.20 Listen to Parts 1 and 2 again and complete the expressions.

Expressing disbelief
1 This is _____!
2 Where on _____ did they get them from?
3 I'm at a loss for _____!

Expressing anger
4 This is o_____!
5 I'm calling to express my _____.
6 Words cannot express my _____.
7 It's totally _____!

b Which two expressions does Victor decide not to use? Why do you think he doesn't use them?

c ▶09.21 Complete the expressions from Parts 1 and 2 with the words or phrases in the box. Add *to* where necessary. Listen and check.

explanation   jump   fulfill your responsibility   right

Commenting on the behavior of others
1 Let's not _____ conclusions.
2 They have no _____!
3 You owe me a(n) _____.
4 You've failed _____ ...

d Which comments in 2c were on Victor's behavior and which were comments on *Free Voice Online's* behavior?

e ▶09.22 Complete the sentences with words from Part 2. Listen and check.

Taking action
1 **I will** _____ the matter.
2 I _____ **you**, there will be consequences.
3 I'd **like to** _____ **in** and we can _____ **it** face to face.

f 💬🔊 Work in pairs. Role-play the conversation between Victor and Aaron using the language in 2a, c, and e. This time Victor should respond positively to Aaron's offer.

3 LISTENING

a ▶ 09.23 Aaron speaks to his employee Leo about using Victor's photos for *Free Voice Online*. Listen to Part 3. What reason does Leo give for Victor's photos being used? What does he want to do?

b ▶ 09.23 Listen to Part 3 again and answer the questions.

1 Why does Aaron want to talk to Victor first?
2 What action does Aaron fear Victor will take?
3 What does Aaron want Leo to do to make up for his mistake?

c 💬🗩 Do you think Aaron has done the right thing? Why / Why not?

4 PRONUNCIATION Sound and spelling: foreign words in English

a ▶ 09.24 Listen to these words. Are they from Spanish, Italian, or French? Which two were in Part 2?

1	avant-garde	5	finito
2	nada	6	tête-à-tête
3	déjà vu	7	rendezvous
4	cappuccino	8	pronto

b Match the words 1–8 in 4a with their meanings a–h.

a ☐ a strange feeling that you have experienced the same thing before
b ☐ an arrangement to meet, usually in secret
c ☐ coffee made with heated, bubbly milk
d ☐ finished
e ☐ nothing
f ☐ different and modern
g ☐ private conversation between two people
h ☐ quickly and without delay

c ▶ 09.24 Listen to the words in 4a again. Underline the consonant sounds that are pronounced in a way that is atypical of English.

d Look at the words in the box. Answer the questions below and then check in a dictionary.

> c'est la vie kaput aficionado faux pas
> kindergarten tsunami paparazzi
> typhoon karaoke siesta

1 What languages do you think these words come from?
2 What do they mean?
3 How are they pronounced by American English speakers?

e ▶ 09.25 Listen and practice saying the words in 4d.

5 SPEAKING

a Work alone. Think of a situation you wish to complain about. Here are some ideas:

- planning permission to build a parking garage across the street from your house has been granted
- the luxury spa vacation you booked and paid for turned out to be in a hostel
- your bank account information has been accessed by hackers.

b 💬🗩 Work in pairs. Take turns being Student A and B. Use your ideas in 5a and the language in 2.

Student A: Explain your situation and complain.

- Express anger and disbelief.
- Comment on B's behavior.
- Respond to B's offer to take action.

Student B: Respond to A's complaint.

- Express understanding of A's situation.
- Comment on A's behavior.
- Offer to take action.

☑ UNIT PROGRESS TEST

→ CHECK YOUR PROGRESS

YOU CAN NOW DO THE UNIT PROGRESS TEST.

1 LISTENING AND SPEAKING

a 💬🔊 Which city in your country has the fastest-growing population? Why do people want to live there?

b 💬🔊 Look at the photos of rural and urban New Zealand. Which environment would you prefer to live in? Why?

c ▶09.26 Listen to Lizzie and Ron talking about life in a rural community in New Zealand compared to life in Auckland, the largest city. Answer the questions.

1 What's Lizzie's news? How is she feeling about it?
2 What point does Ron make about his own and Lizzie's children?
3 What makes it difficult for their children to return to their hometown?
4 Why are Lizzie and Ron better off living where they do?
5 What does Lizzie worry about for the future of their town?

d 💬🔊 What do you think Lizzie, Ron, and their partners should do? Should they stay where they are or follow their children to Auckland? Why?

2 READING

a Read the essay about urban migration. Put these points in the order they are mentioned (1–6).

Urban migration …
☐ has a negative effect on communities in small towns.
☐ is a problem that requires a political solution.
☐ impacts living standards in both cities and small towns.
☐ is driven by work and study needs.
☐ is happening all over the world.
☐ has a negative impact on the supply of city housing.

b 💬🔊 What challenges are there for people who move from small towns or the country to a large city?

Document 1 ↻ 🔍

Urban migration is an international phenomenon. In recent years, *there has been increasing awareness* of issues associated with the migration of people from small towns and rural communities to larger cities. This essay looks at the impact of urban migration on both large cities and rural communities.

Why do people decide to move to a large city? One key factor is that there are often more employment opportunities in urban areas. Secondly, younger people may need to go to a city in order to attend college or other educational programs. Beyond this, others are drawn to cities because of the increased stimulation offered by an urban environment.

The impact on cities [1]*is plain to see*. An increase in population leads to greater demand for housing, causing house prices and rents to rise. As a result, both existing residents and new arrivals in the city are required to spend more of their income on accommodations or are forced to live in substandard conditions.

However, [2]*it could be argued* that the impact on small towns and rural areas is perhaps even greater. A dramatic decrease in the population of rural communities is often due to the number of young people leaving in search of work and study opportunities. This exodus results in the closure of businesses and cutbacks in social services. And those who remain in rural communities suffer a decline in living standards which, in turn, means small communities are seen as even less attractive places to live. As a consequence, towns serving rural communities begin to look like ghost towns.

[3]*By examining* the way urban migration affects both rural and urban communities, [4]*it is evident that* the phenomenon can lead to a decline in living standards for all concerned. [5]*It would seem that* there is a role for governments to play in the way that the movement of population is managed. Intervention such as business incentives and subsidies can ensure small communities continue to offer inhabitants employment opportunities and a good standard of living.

Page 1 of 1   334 words

3 WRITING SKILLS Discussion essays;
Linking: reason and result

a What is the purpose of each paragraph in the essay?

b Notice the phrase in *italics* in the introduction. Does this express the writer's point of view / opinion directly or indirectly? Match the phrases in *italics* (1–5) in the essay with the meanings below.

□□ you can clearly see   □□ I think
□ I've looked

> 💭 **Writing Tip**
>
> When you present a balanced discussion in a formal essay, you should avoid using personal pronouns *I* and *you* and use pronouns like *we*, *it*, and *there*.

c Use the words in the box to complete the formal equivalents; a and b in each pair mean the same thing.

outcome   outlining   noticeable   claimed   appear

1 a I've noticed a slow decline …
  b There has been a slow but _____ decline …
2 a I think it's hard to predict what will happen …
  b The _____ is difficult to predict …
3 a What I'd say is that most residents …
  b It would _____ that most residents …
4 a Now that I've described the issues here …
  b By _____ the issues here …
5 a In my opinion, it's likely …
  b It could be _____ …

d Look at the highlighted examples in the essay in 2a. Which introduce a reason? Which indicate a result? Make two lists.

e Underline the reason or result language in these examples.

1 Urban migration has decreased owing to an increase in grants to rural businesses.
2 There are now many more unemployed people in the city. Consequently, there has been a noticeable increase in small crimes.
3 A drop in living standards causes problems for those at the lower end of the socioeconomic scale.
4 There has been a population increase of 12%. Hence, there has been an increase in new building projects in suburban areas.
5 Some rural workers have returned to the countryside as a direct consequence of the loneliness and isolation of urban life.

f Which expressions in 3e can be used in the same way as these examples?

1 lead to, result in
2 due to, because of
3 As a consequence, As a result

g Choose the correct word in *italics* in these sentences.

1 The increase in new residents in some areas of the city has seen a rise in the number of potential customers for businesses, thereby *creating / create* many new business opportunities.
2 Enrollment in local elementary schools has fallen dramatically. *Thus / Thereby*, many have been closed.
3 Certain local students have gained scholarships to city colleges, *thereby / therefore* freeing their parents from a significant economic burden.

h ≫ Now go to Writing Focus 9D on p. 175.

4 WRITING

a 💬 Think about some kind of social change in your country that is of interest to you, for example:

- demand for college admissions
- involvement in community organizations
- your own idea.

What are the reasons for this change? What are the results? Tell a partner.

b Write a discussion essay about the social change you have chosen. Follow these steps.

- Outline the issue in the introduction.
- Describe reasons for the change and their results.
- Avoid using personal language.
- Hypothesize about the future.
- State whether anything can/should be done about the issue.

c Work with a new partner. Read each other's essays. What kind of social change does your partner's essay talk about? How aware were you of this issue?

UNIT 9
Review and extension

1 GRAMMAR

a Complete the sentences with a reflexive or reciprocal pronoun.

1 I washed the car _myself_ because the car wash was closed.
2 I can see Grandpa is getting old. He seems to talk to _____ all the time.
3 While Simon was in the hospital, his mother was absolutely beside _____.
4 While I'm on vacation, my secretary and I still send _____ several messages a day.
5 We call _____ "The Pirates" because we have a stadium on the coast.
6 Rita and I sat down next to _____ and we looked into _____'s eyes.
7 No one helped us with our house. We built it all by _____.

b Correct one mistake in each sentence or exchange.

1 Kate wanted to put in new windows, but I didn't want.
2 "I'll never listen to her advice again." "So will I."
3 It was a beautiful morning, although was rather cool outside.
4 He living nearby, Frank had no problem getting in early.
5 So they wouldn't get bored, were listening to the radio.
6 "Kelly hasn't read the contract properly." "I don't suspect."
7 She became a famous actress, as her mother.
8 Take the clean mug, not the dirty.

2 VOCABULARY

a Complete the sentences with the words in the box.

recreate	redevelop	regain
reinstate	renovate	restore

1 The city council plans to _____ the wasteland near the port.
2 We will _____ early closing on weekends.
3 The picture was badly damaged, but they managed to _____ it.
4 The aim of *The Oscars* restaurant is to _____ the atmosphere of Hollywood.
5 The town has long been in decline, and I doubt it will ever _____ its former prestige.
6 It took years to _____ the old hotel and modernize all the facilities.

b Choose the best phrase to complete each sentence.

1 ☐ I grew up in a
2 ☐ The nature walk took us to a
3 ☐ Our new office is in a
4 ☐ I work at a
5 ☐ I know a millionaire who owns a
6 ☐ Every city needs an

a power station on the coast.
b subdivision near Dallas.
c mansion in the Caribbean.
d log cabin in the woods.
e iconic skyscraper or two.
f huge building overlooking the river.

3 WORDPOWER *build*

a Look at these multi-word verb collocations with *build*. Match multi-word verbs 1–6 with meanings a–f.

1 **build up** savings / stamina / a following / a reputation
2 **build up to** an announcement / an event / a major change
3 traffic / problems / dirt / pressure **builds up**
4 **build on** our success / strengths / relationship
5 **build in** features (to a product) / activities (to a schedule)
6 **build** something **around** a concept / people

a ☐ use as a basis for the future
b ☐ make an effort to increase
c ☐ use as the main principle/idea
d ☐ include, incorporate
e ☐ increase naturally over time
f ☐ gradually prepare yourself or others for something

b ▶09.27 Complete the sentences with the words in the box. Listen and check.

up (×3)   on   around   in   up to

1 He's **built** this day _____ so much I'm afraid he'll be disappointed.
2 They forgot to **build** _____ auto-locking on this phone.
3 He's **built** _____ a huge fan base over the years.
4 I'm looking for ways to **build** _____ last year's sales.
5 Our business is **built** _____ the idea that people want coffee with their books.
6 What do you think the boss is going to say? She's been **building** _____ a big announcement all week.
7 When the pressure **builds** _____ at work, you need a good, long break.

c Complete each statement with your own idea. Check the meaning of the expressions in **bold** in a dictionary if necessary.

1 People sometimes **build up a tolerance** to _____.
2 I had to **build up the courage** to ask _____.
3 I once **built my hopes up about** _____ but was disappointed.
4 I think **building up a business** would be _____.

d 💬 Compare your answers to 3c with a partner.

⟳ REVIEW YOUR PROGRESS

How well did you do in this unit? Write 3, 2, or 1 for each objective.
3 = very well   2 = well   1 = not so well

I CAN ...	
talk about city life and urban space	☐
describe architecture and buildings	☐
deal with conflict	☐
write a discussion essay.	☐

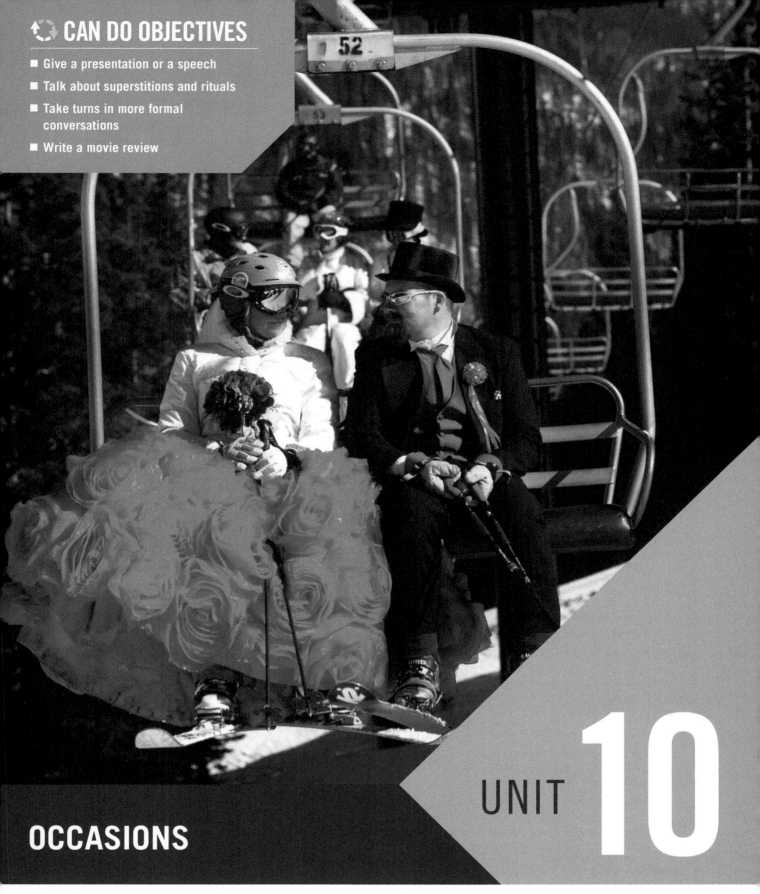

CAN DO OBJECTIVES

- Give a presentation or a speech
- Talk about superstitions and rituals
- Take turns in more formal conversations
- Write a movie review

UNIT **10**

OCCASIONS

GETTING STARTED

a 💬🔊 Look at the picture and answer the questions.

1 Where are these people? What are they doing? How do you think they feel?
2 Why do you think they chose this venue?
3 What do you think happened in the 15 minutes before this picture was taken? What do you think happened afterward?

b 💬🔊 Answer the questions.

1 What's the most memorable wedding you've been to? Why?
2 For you, what are the most important parts of wedding day celebrations?
3 If you could hold a ceremony – such as a wedding – in a unique way, what would you do? Why?

115

10A | I REALLY WISH I'D BEEN ON TIME

Learn to give a presentation or a speech
- G Regret and criticism structures
- V Communication verbs

> If you're not comfortable with public speaking – and nobody starts out comfortable; you have to learn how to be comfortable – practice. I cannot overstate the importance of practicing. Get some close friends or family members to help evaluate you, or somebody at work that you trust.

Hillary Clinton,
politician

> Words mean more than what is set down on paper. It takes the human voice to infuse them with deeper meaning.

Maya Angelou,
poet and civil rights activist

> If you have the opportunity to use your voice, you should use it.

Samuel L. Jackson,
actor

Amy Schumer,
comedian and actor

> Being introverted, it doesn't mean necessarily being shy or being afraid of public speaking; it just means that it's hard for me to interact with people for too long.

1 SPEAKING AND VOCABULARY
Communication verbs

a 💬 Have you ever had to give a speech or presentation? What was the experience like? If not, how would you feel about doing this?

b 💬 Read the quotes. What does each quote tell you about the person's attitude toward giving speeches? Which quotes do you agree with or relate to?

c 💬 What makes a good presentation? What kinds of things can go wrong?

d Read sentences 1–5. Do they mention your ideas in 1c?

1 He kept **making** comments under his breath when he was supposed to be **addressing** the audience.
2 She lost her place whenever she **moved on to** her next point!
3 She **went into** far too much detail and **presented** the information in a confusing way.
4 He **demonstrated** their new approach, but it was pretty boring.
5 He used lots of anecdotes to **illustrate** his points. It was amazing!

e ▶10.01 Find the verbs or verb phrases in **bold** in 1d that collocate with phrases 1–7 below. Listen and check your answers.

1 _____ the results
2 _____ her understanding
3 _____ a conference
4 _____ a different topic
5 _____ the finer points
6 _____ the concept with examples
7 _____ throwaway remarks

f ≫ Now go to Vocabulary Focus 10A on p. 167.

2 READING

a Read Scott Berkun's advice and survival tips on giving presentations and speeches. Which of the four mottos below do you think Berkun would agree with?

1 Take care how you prepare.
2 Feel the fear, go through it, and keep on going.
3 Aim for perfection.
4 Keep explaining again and again until they get it.

b Read the advice and survival tips again. Write notes under the following headings. Compare your ideas with a partner.

1 People's fear of public speaking
2 How fear can help
3 Communicating your ideas effectively
4 Coping with delivery problems
5 Ways to prepare well
6 Understanding your audience

c 💬 Imagine you have to give a talk or presentation. Which piece of Scott Berkun's advice is most relevant for you? Why?

DON'T BE BORING!

How to feel the fear but speak well in public

You've either seen it or you've experienced it yourself: a person standing up in front of a large group. There's no microphone or, if there is, it makes a terrible feedback noise. The person can't be heard, and they say "umm" and "ah" after what seems like every second word. Then they click through their slides too fast and then go back and get themselves in a state of total confusion. Or maybe the projector just gives up the ghost and there are no slides at all.

If this happens to you, you probably feel like you just want to disappear into thin air. If you watch it happen to someone else, you either fall asleep or you desperately want to run from the room. Public speaking can be one of the most terrifying things you have to do in life. But people have to do it all the time – when they study, in their job, and at important events with friends and family.

The fear factor

So, how can you make it better? How can you get over the fear? Scott Berkun, author of *Confessions of a Public Speaker*, suggests that we don't. He thinks we should just own the fear and try and use it to our advantage. There's no doubt that standing up alone in front of a group is never a fun thing to do. It's a little like being in the middle of an open field when you know there are all sorts of dangerous animals nearby. It triggers a classic fear-response scenario that's as old as humankind. Our natural instinct is to run. But, at the same time, our body is pumping adrenaline, and this can give us energy and help us focus. Adrenaline can help us do a good job.

A little narrative goes a long way

Berkun is also a great believer in making sure you have prepared by honing your ideas so that you get them across as effectively as you can. What are the key points you want to make? Work out the most direct way of conveying these to your audience. It's worth remembering that if you wrap your message up in a story, it'll probably have more impact. Storytelling is a very old skill, and audiences usually have a positive response to a message inside a narrative.

Scott Berkun is a writer and public speaker who's interested in a wide range of topics associated with creativity, culture, and business. He studied computer science and philosophy in college and then worked at Microsoft. He now makes his living from his writing and speaking and is the author of the best-selling *Confessions of a Public Speaker*.

Just moving on, folks ...

But how do you respond when things go wrong? Berkun suggests that disaster often invites more disaster. So when you get up to speak, don't apologize for all the things that you don't think are perfect. This starts you off on the wrong foot and doesn't motivate the audience to pay attention to you.

Once you get underway, the trick is just to keep going no matter what happens. If you say you're going to make four points but actually end up making just three, it's likely that almost no one will notice. And if a couple of slides are in the wrong order, just apologize and move on. No one will care that much. Well, you will, but what counts here is what the audience thinks, and they're probably nowhere near as critical as you are.

Even the most accomplished public speakers have good and bad days. And most speakers feel some degree of fear or anxiety at some time. But if you've done your preparation and you greet your audience with confidence, half the battle is won, and your speech will probably be OK!

SCOTT BERKUN'S SURVIVAL TIPS

Berkun's book has a lot of other commonsense tips on how to survive the ordeal of public speaking. Here are some really useful ones:

- Remember the big *R*: research. Make sure that the content of your presentation is thoroughly researched and well planned. This gets you off to a good start.
- Practice, practice, practice. If you practice, you'll be better equipped to deal with unforeseen events while you're speaking – unexpected comments and problems with equipment.

- Don't be boring! This should go without saying, but Berkun continues, "If you are, the worst you'll do is meet expectations." This is great advice because it's so reassuring – you don't have to be exceptional, just good enough.
- Arrive early and sit in one of the chairs that your audience will be in. This will help you empathize with the people you're talking to. They will sense it and like you more as a result.
- Find out what they think: don't forget to ask for feedback after your speech or presentation. Talk to someone who you know will be honest, and listen to what they have to say. This will help you the next time around.

3 LISTENING

a 💬🔊 Which of these, 1 or 2, would you feel more comfortable doing? Why?

1 a presentation for work/school/college
2 a speech for a relative's or friend's birthday/anniversary/wedding

b ▶ 10.03 Listen to three people talk about giving a speech or presentation. Answer the questions.

1 Why were they giving a speech?
2 What went wrong?
3 What was the outcome?

Rob   Chantal   Antonio

c 💬🔊 Answer the questions.

1 Do you think Rob should have refused to be best man? Why / Why not? What's your opinion of Jessica's reaction?
2 What are Chantal's suspicions about the missing file? How likely is it they are correct? How would you react in this situation?
3 How do you think Antonio could have regained control when he got distracted during his talk?

d **Language in context** *Idioms: plans into action*

1 ▶ 10.04 Complete the idioms in **bold** with the words in the box. Then listen and check.

| good | went | threw | recipe |
| yourself | made | out | words |

1 I just _____ **myself into** it.
2 They make me **feel** _____ **of my depth**.
3 I thought I'd **done a** _____ **job on it**.
4 Always make a copy; otherwise it's **a** _____ **for disaster**.
5 I just explained the whole project, and **it** _____ **like clockwork**.
6 The managers were all impressed, and I really _____ **my mark**.
7 I couldn't go on; I was completely **at a loss for** _____.
8 I was sort of saying to myself, "C'mon, **get a grip on** _____!"

2 Match the idioms in 1 with the meanings below.

a ☐ likely to cause serious problems
b ☐ not know what to say
c ☐ do something well
d ☐ regain some self-control when upset or stressed
e ☐ get fully involved in something new
f ☐ go very smoothly without problems
g ☐ impress somebody
h ☐ feel it's too difficult for you

4 GRAMMAR Regret and criticism structures

a Read sentences 1–8. Which sentence does not show a regret?

1 ☐ I should never have agreed to be best man.
2 ☐ If only I'd checked those cards.
3 ☐ Part of me wishes that Dan hadn't asked me to be best man.
4 ☐ I really wish I'd copied the presentation onto my hard drive.
5 ☐ Had he been less underhanded, I might not have the job I have now.
6 ☐ She wasn't my girlfriend, but I used to wish she were.
7 ☐ If I had listened to Teresa's advice, I might have been OK.
8 ☐ If it weren't for my stupidity, we could have raised more money that day.

b Underline the part of each example in 4a that shows regret. Which examples are unreal conditionals?

c ▶ 10.05 **Pronunciation** Mark the word groups and underline the main stress in these two sentences. Listen and check. Practice saying the sentences.

1 If I had listened to Teresa's advice, I might have been OK.
2 If it weren't for my stupidity, we could have raised more money that day.

d ≫ Now go to Grammar Focus 10A on p. 156.

e 💬🔊 What regrets have you had? Talk about one of these past situations.

- a decision to study the wrong subject at school/college
- losing touch with an old friend
- something unfortunate you said to a relative or friend
- a bad decision associated with some kind of social activity

> I wish I hadn't mentioned the family vacation home to my cousin.

> I really regret not replying to her emails.

5 SPEAKING

a Plan a one-minute speech with the title *Learning from My Mistakes*. Talk about a personal experience of some kind. You could develop ideas that you talked about in 4e.

Follow Scott Berkun's advice:

- include an anecdote about your experience to get your point across
- practice your speech several times
- keep going, even if things go wrong.

b 💬🔊 Work in small groups. Deliver your speeches.

Speakers
- Remember to keep still.
- Maintain eye contact with group members.

Listeners
- Think of a question you can ask each speaker about their experiences.

Learn to talk about superstitions and rituals

G Passive reporting verbs
V Superstitions, customs, and beliefs

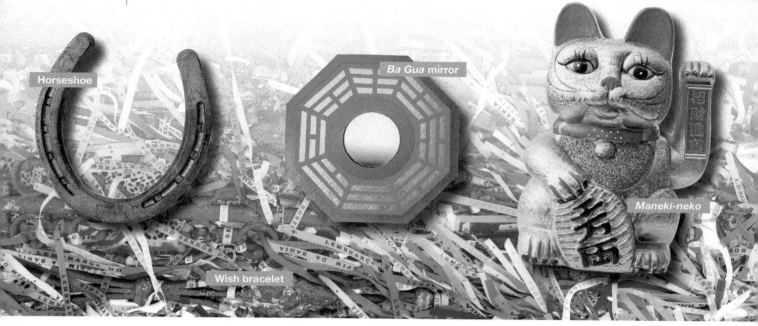

Horseshoe

Ba Gua mirror

Maneki-neko

Wish bracelet

1 SPEAKING AND VOCABULARY
Superstitions, customs, and beliefs

a Look at the objects in the photos.
1 What do you think they all have in common?
2 What part of the world do you think they are from?

b 💬🗨 Which of the objects in 1a do you think these sentences describe?
1 You **make a wish** with every knot you tie.
2 They were **traditionally** nailed above doorways.
3 They stop bad luck entering the house, and they protect it against **magic spells**.
4 It is **customary** to hang them above the front door.
5 It invites **good fortune** and brings wealth to the owner.
6 They are worn as a **good luck charm**.
7 They always face outwards so they can **ward off evil**.

c ▶️ 10.11 Listen and check your answers.

d Look at the words and phrases in **bold** in 1b. Which are connected with ... ?
● luck and magic   ● customs

e ≫ Now go to Vocabulary Focus 10B on p. 168.

f Look at the idiomatic expressions connected with good luck in the box. When do people say them?
1 when they hope something good will happen
2 to warn someone of danger
3 when they're taking extra precautions

fingers crossed   to be on the safe side   knock on wood
third time's the charm   you're tempting fate

g ▶️ 10.14 Complete the sentences with the expressions in 1f. Listen and check.
1 They've agreed to sell the house, so this time next week it'll be ours – _____.
2 I've failed the driving test twice now. Ah well, _____.
3 "I do hope Lisa passes her English exam."
   "Yes, I'll keep my _____."
4 You should wear a bicycle helmet. You've been lucky so far, but _____.
5 I know it's not raining, but take an umbrella just _____.

h ▶️ 10.15 **Pronunciation** Underline the consonant groups in the words in the box in 1f. Remember that these can be across words. Listen and check. Practice saying the expressions.

i 💬🗨 Work in pairs. Take turns being A and B.
Student A: Tell your partner something you're planning to do. Choose from this list.
● go rock climbing   ● take an exam
● apply for a new job   ● travel across Africa by bus
Student B: Respond using a suitable expression from 1f.

Take a guide with you to be on the safe side.

I'm going to climb the Matterhorn.

Good luck. I'll keep my fingers crossed.

j 💬🗨 Answer the questions.
1 Do you know of other things that traditionally bring good luck or ward off evil (in either your own country or another country you know)?
2 How seriously do you think most people believe in charms of this kind? What about you?

2 READING

a 💬🔊 Look at the photo of Uruguayan soccer player Luis Suárez. What do you think he is doing and why?

b Read the introduction to the article to check your answer to 2a. What appear to be the main reasons for this behavior? How effective is it?

c Read the rest of the article and find examples of the rituals 1–7 below. Who performs these rituals? Which one is <u>not</u> mentioned?

1 touching yourself or other people
2 doing things in a particular sequence
3 things that also involve other players
4 lucky objects or clothes
5 particular ways of wearing or putting on clothes
6 things people do on their way to a match
7 things that involve family or friends

d 💬🔊 Which of the rituals do you think is the most "unusual"?

3 GRAMMAR Passive reporting verbs

a Look at the verb forms in **bold**.

1 **It's thought that** performing a "lucky" routine reduces anxiety.
2 Thibaut Courtois **is known to have** an unusual ritual before he plays in an international match.
3 **It is reported that** he has a whole series of rituals that he goes through before every major game.
4 Then he **is believed to send** a selfie to four of his friends in Belgium.
5 He **is said to check** his socks to make sure they are exactly the same height.
6 **It is said that** he never changes this sequence.
7 Before the Olympics, she **is believed to have worn** a pair of "lucky socks."

Why does the writer use passive reporting structures? Two of these answers are correct.

____ to show that they believe the information
____ to show that the information comes from someone else
____ to show that this is not necessarily what they believe

b The sentences in 3a show two structures for reporting information:

a *it* + passive + *that* clause …
b subject + passive + infinitive …

1 Which structure is shown in **bold** in each sentence in 3a, a or b?
2 Which structures in **bold** … ?
   a refer to the present
   b refer to the past
3 How could you express each idea in 3a 1–7 using the other structure?
   Performing a "lucky" routine is thought to reduce anxiety.

THE GAME BEFORE THE GAME

From LUIS SUÁREZ who frequently kisses a tattoo on his hand with the names of his three children, to Serena Williams who bounces the ball exactly five times before she serves and wears the same pair of socks during each match of a tournament – many of the biggest sports stars believe in the power of rituals to bring them luck.

Despite the hours spent training and developing winning strategies, players still go through superstitious rituals just before a big event. It seems nonsensical that such players would give credit for their own success or failure to rituals. However, sports psychologists suggest that these beliefs can actually help players, and in highly competitive sports, this small advantage may mean the difference between winning and losing.

Top Belgian goalkeeper THIBAUT COURTOIS is known to have an unusual ritual before he plays in an international match. While the Belgian national anthem is being played, he always touches his chin. But that's not all. In fact, it is reported that he has a whole series of rituals which he goes through before every major game, not all of them in public. He always enters the stadium corridors at a fixed time. Then he is believed to send a selfie to four of his friends in Belgium. Before going on the field, he always wets the tip of his gloves, and when reaching the goal, he gives the goalpost one kick and then punches the middle of the net. Why does he go through this unusual ritual? He claims that it makes him enter a kind of trance and he can no longer be distracted during the game.

c 💬🔊 The sentences in 3a are typical of news reports and factual writing. How could you say them in a more conversational style?

> People say …

> I've heard …

> Many people think …

d ⫸ Now go to Grammar Focus 10B on p. 157.

The Incredible Rituals That Top Players Perform before a Match

Spanish tennis star RAFAEL NADAL is famous for going through a series of rituals before and during his matches. Before he starts playing, he is said to check his socks to make sure they are exactly the same height. During the game, he always has two water bottles in front of his chair, one behind the other, and during breaks he takes a sip from each bottle in turn. It is said that he never changes this sequence. He also follows exactly the same movements whenever he serves the ball: he touches his foot on the ground behind him, pulls up his shorts, wipes his nose and tucks his hair behind his ears, first on the left side and then on the right. He claims that these rituals are not superstition but a way to give himself a sense of order and of being in control during the match.

The secrets of KAYLA HARRISON's phenomenal success are her rigorous approach to training and a stubborn determination to win. But the U.S. judo Olympic gold medalist also admits to being superstitious and says it's important for her to have rituals and patterns to give her the confidence she needs to win. Before the Olympics, she is believed to have worn a pair of "lucky socks" that were knitted for her by her grandmother, and she decided not to wear a judo outfit that had previously failed to deliver her a win. But there was more than just superstition at play – she combined this with the power of positive thinking. For weeks before the tournament, she visualized herself winning and went meticulously through every step she needed to take on the day of the tournament in order to win.

e Look at these comments about well-known people. Change them so their style would be suitable for a news report using passive reporting structures like those in 3a.
1 They say the goalkeeper is retiring next season.
2 Apparently the manager of the company has resigned.
3 People say she's the best tennis player of all time.
4 The team captain has had eye surgery – or so some people believe.
5 There are rumors that he pulled a muscle in his ankle.

f Think of a well-known person. Write a sentence from a news report about him or her using a passive reporting structure. Then read your sentence aloud. Can other students guess the person?

4 LISTENING

a 💬🎙 Work in groups. Discuss the questions and write down your ideas.
1 Why do you think players go through the rituals described in the article?
2 In what ways do you think rituals might help them?

b ▶ 10.17 Listen to an interview with Sandy Hearst, a sports psychologist. Does she mention any of the points that you noted?

c What is the main point she makes in the interview? Choose 1, 2, or 3.
1 Athletes feel helpless just before a match because they can't influence events, so they need something to make them feel better.
2 Rituals boost athletes' confidence by making them feel more in control, and this makes them perform better.
3 Pre-match rituals have a kind of "magical" effect which can't be explained rationally but which seems to work.

d 💬🎙 ▶ 10.17 Listen to the interview again. Here are some of the things Sandy Hearst says. What do you think she means by the expressions in *italics*?
1 Their behavior may seem *eccentric*.
2 This kind of behavior *makes total sense*.
3 Before a match they are very *hyped up*.
4 Rituals keep their anxiety *at bay*.
5 It's not a *magical effect*.
6 It's like a kind of *placebo effect*.
7 The experiment was *pretty telling*.

5 SPEAKING

a 💬🎙 Think about people you know (or yourself) and write a few notes to answer the questions.
1 Do they do anything you would consider a "ritual"? Think about:
  • routine activities (e.g., getting up, going to work or school)
  • communal activities (e.g., meals, meetings)
  • situations where they need both ability and luck (e.g., taking an exam, sports events).
2 How do you think these "rituals" help them, and why are they important?

b 💬🎙 Work in groups. Use your notes to tell other students about the people you chose.

10C EVERYDAY ENGLISH
Before we move on

Learn to take turns in more formal conversations
- **S** Take turns in an interview
- **P** Intonation in question tags

1 LISTENING

a ▶10.18 Nate receives a phone call from a journalist, Elizabeth, at a student radio station. Listen to Part 1. Why is Elizabeth calling? What is Nate's reaction?

b ▶10.18 Listen to Part 1 again and answer the questions.
1 Why does Nate say that he doesn't want to donate money?
2 What does Elizabeth say she *isn't* doing?
3 What word does Elizabeth use to describe Nate's hike? What does it mean?

c 💬🗣 Look at the photo below. Do you think Elizabeth was satisfied with the call? Do you think Nate is interested in doing the interview? Explain your answers.

d ▶10.19 Nate agrees to be interviewed on air by Elizabeth. Listen to Part 2 and put the items in the order they're mentioned.

a ☐ Nate's father   c ☐ Nate's inspirations
b ☐ Nate's hike   d ☐ Nate's hometown

e ▶10.19 Listen to Part 2 again and take notes on the points in 1d.

f 💬🗣 Do you think the interview has been successful? Why / Why not?

2 USEFUL LANGUAGE Turn-taking

a Match the expressions in **bold** with their uses a–c. Some expressions have more than one use.
1 **Sorry, if I could just finish** what I was saying, Nate.
2 **Sorry to interrupt, but** that is so inspiring.
3 **Speaking of which,** you grew up here in Seattle, didn't you?
4 **Please, after you.**
5 **As I was saying,** I never forgot those first camping trips.
6 **If you don't mind me cutting in here,** you had to do a lot of preparation for this hike, didn't you?

a interrupt someone and take a turn speaking
b encourage someone else to speak
c continue speaking about the same subject

b When would you use these phrases in a conversation?
1 **Go on.**
2 **Before we get started …**
3 **Before we move on …**

c ▶10.20 Complete the conversation with the expressions in 2a and 2b. There may be more than one correct answer. Listen and check.

A So, I understand you're a motivational speaker.
B That's right. Basically I go to company conferences and give talks on …
A ¹_____ where are these conferences?
B Oh, all over the country. Overseas sometimes, too. But ²_____, companies employ me to talk about my mountaineering adventures to share a message of drive and ambition.
A And I don't suppose you imagined when you started mountaineering that you would end up doing this.
B No, I …
A I mean, did you think …
B Sorry?
A No, I'm sorry. ³_____.
B Well, no. I never imagined I would be going around speaking at conferences …
A ⁴_____ you have some really exciting stories of your mountaineering days, don't you?
B ⁵_____ what I was saying. I never imagined speaking at conferences, but I'd like to say that I've been amazed at the warm welcome I've received in the business world.
A That's good to hear. Now, …

d 💬🗣 Practice the interview in 2c with a partner, but change the profession of the interviewee.

3 LISTENING

a ▶ 10.21 Listen to Part 3 and choose the best answer to the questions.

1 Why is Elizabeth pleased?
   a She did a great interview with a difficult interviewee.
   b She's finally getting the credit she is due.
   c She feels exhilarated after a successful broadcast.
   d Nate is going to write a blog post about her.

2 What does Nate think Elizabeth did that helped the interview?
   a She spoke politely.
   b She asked good questions.
   c She sent him the questions in advance.
   d She mentioned his charity.

3 What are Elizabeth and Nate going to do together?
   a have lunch the next day
   b have another interview after the book comes out
   c go on a hike over the summer
   d start doing weekly interviews at the station

b 💬 Who would you like to interview? Think about someone who is famous or someone who has inspired you. Say why you would like to talk to this person and what questions you would ask.

c ▶ 10.22 Language in context *Praising idioms* Match the two halves of the idioms. Listen and check.

1 ☐ Well, credit where   a your praises.
2 ☐ Hats off   b to you.
3 ☐ Everyone has   c best thing since
   been singing   sliced bread.
4 ☐ You're the   d credit's due.

4 PRONUNCIATION Intonation in question tags

a ▶ 10.23 Listen to the sentences from Parts 2 and 3. Does the intonation rise (↗) or fall (↘) on each question tag in **bold**?

1 You grew up here in Seattle, **didn't you?**
2 You had to do a lot of preparation for this hike, **didn't you?**
3 It's really the cherry on top, **isn't it**, Nate**?**

b Complete the rules with *rising* or *falling*.

- If you're not sure what you've said is correct, use a _____ intonation on the question tag.
- If you know what you've said is correct and you want the other person to confirm it, use a _____ intonation on the question tag.

c ▶ 10.24 Listen to these questions and say which intonation you hear – A (↗) or B (↘).

1 You did, didn't you?   4 They do, don't they?
2 You can't, can you?   5 I should, shouldn't I?
3 She hasn't, has she?   6 It will, won't it?

d 💬 Work in pairs. Take turns saying a sentence from 4c, using different intonations for the question tag. Your partner says *A* or *B*.

e 💬 We often use a question tag with a falling intonation after giving an opinion in order to elicit agreement from the person we are speaking to. Give your opinions on the topics below and elicit your partner's agreement using a question tag.

- a strange superstition
- a famous athlete
- a good TV documentary

5 SPEAKING

a Work on your own. Pretend you are a famous athlete. Answer the questions. Make up answers if you do not know the correct answers.

1 What's your name and hometown?
2 What's your sports background and what team do you play for / who is your sponsor?
3 What unusual superstitious rituals do you have? (Think of three.) Here are some ideas:
   - lucky charms   - pre-game routine   - particular clothing

b You are going to interview your partner in their role as a famous athlete. Think of some questions to ask them.

c 💬 Work with a partner. Take turns interviewing each other. Think of answers to your partner's questions. Use expressions for turn-taking and question tags.

✓ UNIT PROGRESS TEST

→ CHECK YOUR PROGRESS

YOU CAN NOW DO THE UNIT PROGRESS TEST.

10D SKILLS FOR WRITING
The movie is a visual feast

1 SPEAKING AND LISTENING

a 💬📢 What makes you want to see a movie? Choose one or more from the following or your own idea.

> seeing a trailer   reading a plot synopsis
> reading a review   having read the book
> hearing a friend's recommendation

b Read the descriptions of the movie *Ad Astra* and match them to the places you would find them.

1 ☐ on a movie download website
2 ☐ on a customer review website
3 ☐ on a sign outside a movie theater
4 ☐ in a critic's review online

c 💬📢 How much are you influenced by reviews? Is there a reviewer whose judgment you trust? What are the reasons for and against reading reviews?

d ▶10.25 Listen to four people talking about how they use reviews. Take notes to answer the questions.

1 What kind of movie reviews do they read? Why?
2 When do they read them?
3 Do they read any other kinds of reviews?

Which person's opinions are closest to your own?

e 💬📢 What other kinds of reviews do you find useful? What kinds of reviews have you written yourself?

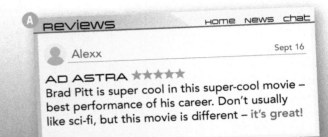

A **Reviews**   Home   News   Chat

👤 Alexx   Sept 16

AD ASTRA ★★★★★
Brad Pitt is super cool in this super-cool movie – best performance of his career. Don't usually like sci-fi, but this movie is different – it's great!

B **Ad Astra** 2019
Astronaut Roy McBride is sent to Mars to communicate with his father in outer space. The father is sending dangerous power surges through the solar system. From Mars, McBride hijacks a spaceship because he wants to confront his father face-to-face.

Buy Movie $9.99   Rent Movie $4.99

C **Review**

Although they only have small cameo roles, Tommy Lee Jones and Donald Sutherland give memorable performances. They both give a master class in creating complex characters in limited screen time.

Read More

D **NOW SHOWING AD ASTRA**

"**Mesmerizing** and **electrifying**. James Gray directs an instant classic."

– Movie Review Magazine

2 READING

a Read two reviews of *Ad Astra*. Which reviewer is more positive? What are the main differences in their feelings about the movie?

b 💬 Based on these two reviews alone, would you want to see the movie? Why / Why not?

Review   Ad Astra

Director James Gray makes his first venture into sci-fi with *Ad Astra*. It's a thought-provoking movie reminiscent of sci-fi classics such as *2001: A Space Odyssey* and *Alien*. Brad Pitt plays Roy McBride, an astronaut with the ability to keep his cool in dangerous situations. Having survived a dangerous fall in space, he is sent on a top-secret mission to stop a series of outer space power surges that are causing chaos on Earth.

It's believed the power surges are linked to another mission, Project Lima. This mission, led by McBride's father, Clifford (Tommy Lee Jones), was a failed exploration for intelligent life at the edges of the solar system. Fearing that Clifford is still alive and has gone rogue, the authorities only want Roy to make contact with his father from Mars. But he has different ideas, and the movie promises to be a father-son showdown in outer space.

Some moviegoers may find *Ad Astra* slower paced than some sci-fi movies, but it's not without its exciting sequences. And this is Brad Pitt's best performance in years. While his character seems emotionally detached from other people, Pitt manages to convey a depth of feeling with enormous subtlety.

For me, the strength of *Ad Astra* lies in the way it blends sci-fi with intense personal feeling. It's really a classic family drama about a son needing to escape from the shadow of the father. This won't appeal to some die-hard sci-fi fans only interested in action and thrills. But, to my mind, it makes the movie more textured and more interesting. *Ad Astra* is set to become a classic.

AD ASTRA   Review

Director James Gray has assembled a stellar cast for his latest movie, *Ad Astra*. Brad Pitt is joined by veteran actors Tommy Lee Jones and Donald Sutherland, and they're working from a script written by Gray together with Ethan Gross.

Brad Pitt plays Roy McBride, an astronaut sent on a mission to outer space to get in touch with his father, Clifford McBride (Tommy Lee Jones), also an astronaut. McBride Senior seems to have gone crazy and is suspected of sending chaotic power surges back to Earth.

Things get off to an exciting start when Roy McBride (Brad Pitt) is thrown off a tower in space and almost falls to his death. We meet him next in a hospital bed reflecting on his psychological condition. This is where the movie starts to get bogged down. There's a little too much psychology, and it gets in the way of what could have been a great intergalactic thrill ride.

Ad Astra looks great, but the storyline feels a bit like a reworking of sci-fi movies we've seen before. However, there are some lovely and amusing touches like the $120 hot face towels on the commercial flight to the moon. Brad Pitt looks the part of an ace astronaut, but he comes across distant and remote. He's not the kind of hero that you really want to root for – we need less reflection and more action.

Overall, I enjoyed the movie and it kept me engaged. But I often wanted to hurry things along, and I wasn't sitting on the edge of my seat in the way that a good sci-fi movie makes you. But if you like your sci-fi together with psychology and stunning visual images, then *Ad Astra* is worth a look.

3 WRITING SKILLS
Movie reviews; Concise description

a Check (✓) the elements that are included in the reviews. Are they included in the same order in both reviews?

1 ☐ when and where the writer saw the movie
2 ☐ the names of the director and actors
3 ☐ outline of the plot
4 ☐ how the movie ends
5 ☐ strong points of the movie
6 ☐ weak points of the movie
7 ☐ short summarizing statement
8 ☐ recommendation – whether to see it or not

Should the elements you didn't check be included in a review? Why / Why not?

b Which reviewer mentions strengths or weaknesses in the following areas? Write *A*, *B*, or *both*.

1 plot   3 acting   5 themes/messages
2 characters   4 filming   6 success of the movie

c Underline three expressions the writers use to write about movies that you would find useful to learn. Compare with other students. Did you choose the same ones?

d Compare the excerpts below with the first two paragraphs of Review A. How are the words in *italics* different in Review A? Why do you think the writer of Review A chose to do this? Choose 1 or 2.

1 to make the meaning more explicit
2 to give the information more concisely

After he has survived a dangerous fall in space …
This mission, *which was led* by McBride's father, Clifford …
Because they are afraid that Clifford is still alive and has gone rogue …

e ≫ Now go to Writing Focus 10D on p. 175.

4 WRITING

a Choose a movie or TV series you know and plan a review of 220–260 words. Think about:
• describing the movie or TV series for someone who hasn't seen it
• main strengths and weaknesses
• how to structure your review into four paragraphs.

b Write the review. Try to:
• use adjectives to give an intense description
• make the information as concise as possible.

c Read another student's review. Do you know the movie or TV series? If so, decide if you agree with what it says. If not, decide whether you'd like to see it based on the review.

UNIT 10
Review and extension

1 GRAMMAR

a Complete the sentences with the words in the box.

have   it   shouldn't   only   ought to   rather   time   wish

1 You could _____ asked me before getting involved.
2 I would _____ you spoke to Jean about it.
3 _____ was revealed that the manager had resigned.
4 If _____ everyone were as generous as you.
5 It's _____ the government did something about crime.
6 I _____ you would behave when my friends come over.
7 You _____ look at me with a face like that.
8 Harriet _____ feel ashamed of herself.

b Rewrite the sentences using the words in parentheses.

1 Why didn't you call me? (should)
2 It wasn't necessary for you to meet me. (didn't need)
3 They say that the president owns a private zoo. (said)
4 It's a shame we don't live closer. (wish)
5 There's no way that Alex was on time. (couldn't)
6 It was a bad idea for Sarah to lose her temper. (If only)
7 People think that she died in a car crash. (thought)

2 VOCABULARY

a Match the sentence halves 1–6 with endings a–f.

1 ☐ The president concluded
2 ☐ It is important to back
3 ☐ I would also like to pay
4 ☐ There's no time to go into
5 ☐ Before we move on to
6 ☐ You also need to sell

a tribute to a dear friend, Carlos Sanchez.
b the idea to your audience.
c up arguments with solid facts.
d the finer points, so I'll leave it there.
e her speech with some words of thanks.
f a different topic, let me summarize.

b Complete the missing words.

1 Good luck in the race. I'll keep my f_____ crossed.
2 We've lost twice already. Third t_____ the charm!
3 That might be t_____ fate.
4 I find Tracey's story c_____ and will support her.
5 To be on the safe s_____, let's go by taxi.
6 Blow out the candles and m_____ a wish.

3 WORDPOWER *luck* and *chance*

a ▶ 10.26 Replace the words in *italics* with the correct phrases in the box. Listen and check.

a fighting chance   blow my chances   on the off chance
don't stand a chance   it's tough luck   're in luck
consider yourself lucky

1 I can't believe what you said in that meeting! You should *be relieved* that nobody was listening.
2 We're inviting you *because there's a small possibility* that you're free that night.
3 The treatment is essential to give him *a possibility of recovering*.
4 I'm sorry you don't like the situation, Mark, but *you'll have to put up with it*, I'm afraid.
5 I always *destroy any possibility of success* in interviews because I get so nervous.
6 You know that book you wanted to borrow? Well, you *can do that now*! I found it under the bed.
7 Their top player is out with an injury, and without him they *have no possibility of winning*.

b ▶ 10.27 Complete the exchanges using the correct forms of the phrases in 3a. Use one word in each blank. Listen and check.

1 **A** I can't believe I missed the entry date for applications. I've really _____ my chances there.
    B Why don't you send it in anyway, _____ the _____ chance they're still recruiting?
2 **A** Do you have the notes from yesterday's lecture?
    B You're _____ luck. That's the first lecture I've taken notes at this year. Here you go.
3 **A** It's six o'clock already. I don't _____ a chance of getting this homework finished tonight.
    B _____ luck, I'm afraid. I'm not helping you.
4 **A** I'm so worried about how badly I did on those exams.
    B Well, _____ yourself lucky that everyone else did badly, too. At least you have a _____ chance of getting a decent grade.

c 💬 What could you say to these people using the expressions in 3a? (There is more than one answer.)

• a friend who missed the bus
• a busy person you'd like to meet with
• someone who wants to borrow some money from you
• a friend who should go to bed because they have a test the next day
• a friend who lost their wallet but got it back

⟳ REVIEW YOUR PROGRESS

How well did you do in this unit? Write 3, 2, or 1 for each objective.
3 = very well   2 = well   1 = not so well

I CAN ...	
give a presentation or a speech	☐
talk about superstitions and rituals	☐
take turns in more formal conversations	☐
write a movie review.	☐

This page is intentionally left blank.

6A

a Look at the photos from a photography competition. Why do you think each photo won a prize? Use the adverbs and adjectives from the box and your own ideas to talk about the photos with a partner.

Adverbs

truly utterly incredibly completely absolutely
extremely rather a little pretty quite gently
wonderfully very

Adjectives

well-composed powerful meaningful gritty
raw playful humorous evocative exotic iconic
nonsensical sensational bleak flawless ironic
elaborate cluttered

> This is an utterly sensational image. It really draws you in.

> Yes, it's quite evocative. It makes me think of …

b Which photo do you think should be the overall winner of the competition? Why? Agree on one image with your partner.

c ⟫ Now go to p. 70.

7C STUDENT B

a Conversation 1 Read your first card. Think about what you might say using the language on p. 87. Then listen to Student A and reply.

1
- You had arranged to meet Student A at the movie theater to see a movie you'd been wanting to see.
- The appointment slipped your mind completely.
- You went out with another friend to a restaurant instead. Your cell phone had run out of battery.
- On your way out of the restaurant, you saw Student A across the street. You suddenly remembered your appointment and decided to pretend you hadn't seen them.
- When you got home and recharged your battery, you received an angry text from Student A.
- You realize that you were in the wrong and feel very ashamed. You hope you can still be friends.

b Conversation 2 Now look at your second card. Think about what you want to say. Then start the conversation with Student A.

2
- You requested a promotion at work. Anxious about it, you told one of your coworkers, Student A, in confidence.
- You got the promotion!
- While congratulating you, another coworker let slip that they'd known you'd requested the promotion for some time.
- You realize that Student A must have told her, but it doesn't matter now anyway.

9B STUDENT A

a Start a conversation with Student B. Listen to Student B and reply using the ideas below in order. Use ellipsis and substitution to make the conversation natural.

1 I don't like our neighborhood anymore.
3 I'm glad you agree. They're knocking down all the beautiful old buildings, and they're putting up ugly new buildings.
5 It's terrible, isn't it? And they said they were going to restore the old town hall, but they haven't restored the old town hall yet.
7 It's all a big mess. I really want to do something, but it's hard to know what to do.
9 Yes, starting an online petition to save the town hall is a good idea. And we could hold a protest.
11 You're right. It probably would be taking things a little too far. We'll start with the petition.

b Now go to p. 108.

9A STUDENT A

a Read the fact file and prepare to tell other students about the situation.

EXHIBITION ROAD, LONDON, UK

- A busy street turned into "shared space"
- Street is shared between vehicles and pedestrians
- Traffic signs, safety barriers removed; trees and benches added

AIMS AND ACHIEVEMENTS

- Traffic is reduced and moves more slowly
- Drivers take more responsibility and drive more carefully because there are no signs telling them what to do
- Drivers and pedestrians make eye contact with each other
- Safety is improved and pedestrians have more space to move

b Now go back to p. 105.

a Read the fact file and prepare to tell other students about the event.

BANKJESCOLLECTIEF (BENCHES COLLECTIVE),
MONTHLY EVENT IN WARMER MONTHS, AMSTERDAM

FACT FILE

- Residents and businesses bring a bench to the street from which they offer food or other activities
- Visitors to the bench pay what they think the offering is worth

AIMS AND ACHIEVEMENTS

- To transform Amsterdam into the biggest outdoor café in the world
- People get the opportunity to meet their neighbors and enter into spontaneous interactions
- People become comfortable in the city as a place they own and influence, like their living room

- Beyond food and drink, benches have included: story-telling, salsa classes, knitting workshops, and clothing swap sessions

b Now go back to p. 105.

9B **STUDENT B**

a Student A will start a conversation with you. Listen and reply using the ideas below. Use ellipsis and substitution to make the conversation natural.

> 2 I don't like our neighborhood anymore. A lot of people think it's OK, but I don't think it's OK.
> 4 That's right. They've just gone ahead and they have built that horrible new supermarket and they have put up the ugly new sports center.
> 6 They'll probably knock it down, but they shouldn't knock it down.
> 8 We could start an online petition to save the town hall.
> 10 Do you think we ought to hold a protest? It might be taking things a little too far.

b Now go to p. 108.

9A **STUDENT C**

a Read the fact file and prepare to tell other students about the situation.

Suburban bus stop makeover, Pittsburgh, PA

- Revamp a bus stop on a busy highway

Aims and achievements

- Long-term, provide a bus stop where people would actually want to sit
- Create shelter from unpleasant weather
- Increase the distance from the road so pedestrians feel safe
- Reduce the risk of crime by lighting the surrounding area
- For the opening, colorful soft furnishings were used to decorate the bus stop

b Now go back to p. 105.

9A STUDENT D

a Read the fact file and prepare to tell other students about the situation.

CONGRESS SQUARE PARK, PORTLAND, ME

• Community organization formed to save a public space

AIMS AND ACHIEVEMENTS

• Restore public faith in the safety of the area

• Re-popularize the square

• Local residents cleaned up the area

• People brought furniture and street food stalls, free Wi-Fi

• More and more people used the square

• Protected land from being sold to developers

b Now go back to p. 105.

7D

a Read about two different team-building programs. Which one would be more appropriate for your team? Why?

Adventure team building

We will take your team hiking in the great outdoors. Our activities develop:
• **real-life survival skills**
• **cooperation and communication skills**
• **self-awareness and mutual respect.**
Ideal for building a really strong team.

 Personal Adventures

Action team building

We have a fantastic range of action games that develop better team dynamics. The games are chosen to foster problem-solving abilities and promote active listening and effective, positive communication among team members.

These physical activities are great fun and really safe – no special abilities are necessary!

Let your team remember the joy of being a child while learning how to work together.

Action Stations Development

b Now go back to p. 89.

7C STUDENT A

a **Conversation 1** Read your first card. Think about what you want to say. Then start the conversation with Student B.

1
• You had arranged to meet Student B at the movie theater to see a movie you'd been wanting to see.
• Since Student B has a reputation for being late, you had bought the tickets in advance for yourself and Student B.
• You waited for a long time, but Student B didn't show up despite the fact that you texted and called.
• You went to see what was left of the movie on your own, and on your way home you saw Student B leaving a restaurant.
• You shouted and waved, but Student B seemed to be ignoring you. You now feel very hurt and angry and don't think your friendship has much future.

b **Conversation 2** Now look at your second card. Think about what you want to say using the language on p. 87. Listen to Student B and reply.

2
• A coworker, Student B, had confided in you about a promotion they'd asked for.
• Another coworker also told you that she had requested a promotion and that she was absolutely certain she'd get it because there was no one else in the office with her skills and capabilities.
• In the heat of the moment, you told her that Student B had also gone in for the promotion and that to your mind, Student B was the stronger candidate.
• Afterward, you realized that you shouldn't have betrayed Student B's confidence, and you feel terrible.

GRAMMAR FOCUS

6A Simple and continuous verbs

▶ 06.05 Simple verbs

We use simple verbs to talk about complete actions, events, or activities:

*I'**ve just taken** an amazing picture of two foxes.*
*We **trained** really hard for the marathon we **ran** in April.*

We use a simple verb when we say how much is complete or how many times something happens:

*I **went** to the Museum of Modern Art three times last year.*
*We **got** about half the work done.*

We use simple verbs to talk about facts and unchanging states:

*The camera **takes** up to ten photos per second in this mode.*
*My dad **was born** in Mexico City and **has never left**.*

▶ 06.06 Continuous verbs

We use continuous verbs to talk about incomplete or temporary activities:

*Brian **was trying** to take a picture, but someone got in the way.*
*I'm on a temporary contract, so I'**m** only **working** here for six months.*

We use continuous verbs to emphasize activity, duration, or repetition:

*I'**m going** to classes to improve my photography.*
*In March, we **will have been living** here for four years.*
*Mandy **has been calling** me all day and **telling** me what to do.*

We can use continuous verbs with the adverbs *always, continually, constantly,* and *forever* to complain or express surprise about how frequently something happens:

*James **was constantly taking** photos of every little thing he saw.*
*It'**s always raining** in this part of the world.*

> ### 💬 Tip
> We can use the past continuous to be more polite or less direct:
> *I **was hoping** I could borrow your camera.*
> *Thank you for a lovely evening. It's time we **got going**.*

Verbs not usually used in the continuous

Some verbs are almost never used in the continuous, e.g., *know* and *suppose*:

*I **have known** Nina for ages.* NOT ~~am knowing~~
*I **don't suppose** you know where the paints are?* NOT ~~'m not supposing~~

Below are some verbs that are not usually used in the continuous:

Thinking
believe, despise, know, recognize, regard, suppose, realize *I'm sure Trevor **despises** everything we are trying to do.* NOT ~~is despising~~

The senses*
hear, see, smell, sound, taste *We **have seen** a brilliant performance from Ronaldo.* NOT ~~have been seeing~~

Communicating
astonish, deny, impress, mean, satisfy, take (= understand) *Nothing about his behavior that day **impressed** me.* NOT ~~was impressing~~

Other
belong, consist, depend, fit, possess *The corner office now **belongs** to you.*

*We use *can* + an ability verb like *hear, remember, see, taste* rather than a continuous form:

*I **can hear** somebody coming.* NOT ~~I am hearing~~

Verbs with different meanings in the simple and continuous

*Rachel **weighs** 170 pounds.* (a state)	*Rachel **is weighing** herself.* (an activity)
*What **do** you **think** about digital cameras?* (an opinion)	*I'**m thinking** of going to art school.* (an activity)
*Ella **is** a difficult child.* (a characteristic)	*Ella'**s being** difficult.* (behavior)
*What can you **see** in this picture?* (see = look at) *Do you **see** what I mean?* (see = understand)	*The doctor **is seeing** a patient.* (see = meet)

a Match the sentences with the pictures.

1

a Chiara ate the chocolate.
b Chiara was eating the chocolate.

2

a Simon took a bath.
b Simon was taking a bath.

3

a Sam is a doctor.
b Sam is being a doctor.

4

a Nina comes from Russia.
b Nina is coming from Russia.

b Choose the best option.

1 I *think* / *'m thinking* photography is more about technology than art.
2 I'll *be learning* / *learn* English for the rest of my life.
3 *Are you* / *Are you being* obstinate just to annoy me?
4 Everyone had *left* / *been leaving*, and there was complete silence.
5 Jon *thinks* / *'s thinking* of joining the army next year.
6 *Do you realize* / *Are you realizing* how this makes me look?
7 Someone has *been gossiping* / *gossiped* and I'm really upset.
8 Unemployment *increases* / *is increasing*, but the government doesn't care.
9 We *opened* / *were opening* our first office in summer 2012.
10 I *suppose* / *'m supposing* we'll have to wait for the bus.

c Complete the text with either the simple or continuous form of the verbs in parentheses.

Roma So do you ¹ _think_ (think) graffiti could be called art?

Judy Why not? Graffiti has a long tradition, and we know the Romans ² _____ (have) it.

R Yes, but people have ³_____ (complain) about graffiti for a long time, too. I must admit that every time I ⁴_____ (see) a wall covered in the stuff, it annoys me.

J Well, obviously you have ⁵_____ (decide) that real art ⁶_____ (belong) in museums and nowhere else. Graffiti is the most natural form of street art there is. Haven't you ⁷_____ (watch) that series on TV lately about popular art? It has ⁸_____ (change) my idea of art for good. Actually, I have always ⁹_____ (want) to be good at art.

R What ¹⁰_____ (say)? Are you going to go out and paint some graffiti on a train station wall?

J No, I don't think train passengers would think much of that.

d ⟫⟫⟫ Now go back to p. 70.

6B Participle clauses

We use participle clauses to add more information to a sentence:
Hiding behind the bushes, I held my breath.
The stranger staggered into the room, *shaking and covered in snow*.

Participle clauses after nouns

We can sometimes use participle clauses after nouns and pronouns. They are similar to defining relative clauses that have continuous and passive verbs. Look at the following examples:
We found the wallet (that was) *lying by the side of the road*.
Everybody (who had been) *affected by the fire* was told to leave their homes.
The streets were full of people (who were) *dancing for joy*.
Alice in Wonderland *was the book* (that was) *chosen* by the majority of students.
Joanna is a *woman who says* what she thinks. NOT ~~woman saying~~
(*says* is not a continuous verb)
The *building that collapsed* was to be rebuilt. NOT ~~building collapsed~~
(*collapsed* is not a passive)
The subject of a participle clause must be the same as the main clause:
The *boat* that we were waiting for was late. NOT ~~the boat waiting for~~

> **Tip**
> We can use participle clauses with verbs not usually used in continuous tenses:
> *You will come to a large rock resembling a castle.* = rock that resembles a castle NOT ~~rock that is resembling~~
> *I wasn't sure where to go, not being a local.*

Participle clauses as adverbials

We use participle clauses as adverbials in formal language and writing:
Approaching an intersection, I observed a car making an illegal turn.
Left by themselves, young children can get into all sorts of trouble.
Adverbial participle clauses say why, when, where, and how:
Frightened by what he saw, he never returned.
= Because he was frightened …
Having thought it over, I've decided to refuse their offer.
= Because I've thought about it …
Stopping for a break, we discussed what to do next.
= After we stopped …
Standing by the fire, Mary thought about her next step.
= While she stood …
Climbing out of the window, he managed to escape. = By climbing …
Using my knife, I forced the box open. = With my knife …

Participle clauses always start before or at the same time as the main verb in the sentence:
The man *running alongside me* tripped and fell.
Sensing I was being watched, I looked into the shadows.
We can make it very clear a participle clause begins earlier by using the perfect form:
Having finally found a job, I called my parents with the happy news.
Not having seen the incident, I'm not the best person to tell you what happened.

> **Tip**
> We can use -ed adverbial participle clauses after time conjunctions in formal language:
> *When faced with danger*, most people would just panic.
> The vacation of a lifetime! *Once experienced*, it will never be forgotten.

Standing as still as he could, he waited for the next throw.

a Check (✓) the correct sentences. Correct the mistakes you found in the remaining sentences.

1 ☐ ~~Tony~~ R running at full speed, he managed to jump on the train.
2 ☐ Remembering my appointment, I jumped up and left.
3 ☐ I will find the person committed this crime.
4 ☐ There was a terrible smell coming from the room.
5 ☐ Offering to pay for the damage, he had caused the accident.
6 ☐ Reading the letter, my hands were shaking in excitement.
7 ☐ Not belonging to the group, I felt very out of place.
8 ☐ Johnny is the kind of man never arriving anywhere on time.

b Complete the beginning of the story with the participle clauses in the box.

> being realistic   coming outside   ~~following me~~
> being overworked and underpaid   getting stressed out
> waiting to strike   wearing orange

I knew that there was a man[1] *following me*. That morning, [2]_____, I saw him again. The strange thing was that he made no effort to hide; [3]_____, he seemed to want to be seen. Anyway, [4]_____, what could I do? [5]_____, the local police would hardly have time to listen to my suspicions. It wasn't exactly the crime of the century, either. Maybe it was just me [6]_____ as a result of too much work. As things turned out, my stalker, [7]_____, was a very serious threat indeed.

c Rewrite the next part of the story using participle clauses where possible.
Sitting down,
I went to the café on the street corner. ~~I sat down and~~ I ordered a piece of cake. A piece of cake that was covered in chocolate was quickly brought over to my table. I noticed something that was sticking out from under the cake, so I lifted it up. Underneath I found a note that was written in red that said, "Get into the car that is waiting across the road." I was frightened by the tone and I feared the worst, so I did what the note said. A thousand negative thoughts were crowding my head when I got to the car. The familiar figure who was dressed in orange was in the front seat, with a sinister smile on his face. "We meet at last," he said.

d ≫ Now go back to p. 73.

▶ **07.05** **Certain speculations: *will* / *going to***

We use *will* to speculate with certainty about the future. We add *have* + past participle to speculate about past actions with an effect on the present. We use *going to* for strong predictions based on present evidence. We often use adverbs with *will* and *going to* to modify the degree of certainty:

*Paper books **probably won't** disappear altogether.*
*I'm sure she **will have arrived** by now. Let's go and see.*
*It's a terrible movie! It's **hardly going to** win an Oscar.*

▶ **07.06** **Certain deductions: *must* / *have got to***

We use *must* and *have got to* (informal) to say something is logically true in the present and future (make a deduction based on evidence). We use *must* + *have* + past participle to deduce about the past:

*Lisa is all dressed up. She **must be going** somewhere nice.*
*Joy didn't hear the phone. She **must have been sleeping**.*
*I don't believe it! You**'ve got to be joking**.*

▶ **07.07** **Likely: *should* / *may well***

We use *should* about the past, present, and future to say that something is probable because it is normal and expected. *May well* is slightly more certain than *should*:

*It's 6:00, so they **should have arrived** by now. / **should be arriving** soon.*
*Solar power **may well be** the answer to our energy problems.*

▶ **07.08** **Possible and unlikely: *could* / *might* / *may* / *can***

We use *could*, *may* (*not*), and *might* (*not*) both to speculate and deduce in the past, present, and future:

*Fuel **could**/**may** (**not**)/**might** (**not**) run out in the near future.* NOT ~~can~~
*Jill is late. She **could**/**might**/**may have gotten** lost. She **could**/**might**/**may be wandering** around out there.* NOT ~~can~~

We also use *could* + *have* + past participle to say what was hypothetically possible in the past:

*I didn't know you were in town. We **could have met** up.*
We use *can* to say that something is generally possible in the present/future:
*You **can** see bears in the woods at this time of the year.*

▶ **07.09** **Impossible: *can't* / *couldn't***

Couldn't + base form says what was generally impossible in the past. *Can't* + base form says what is generally impossible in the present and future. We also use *can't*/*couldn't* + *have* + past participle (past) or *can't* + *be* (+ verb + -*ing* / *going to*) (present/future) to say something is logically impossible:

*They **couldn't get** here yesterday. They **can't get here** today or tomorrow.* = impossible
*The exam **can't**/**couldn't have been** very difficult if you finished in 20 minutes.* = logically impossible
*Jeffrey **can't be working** on a Sunday evening. The building's closed.*
Couldn't + *have* + past participle also says what was impossible in the hypothetical past:

*I **couldn't have passed** the exam without Peter's help.* (= I passed because of his help; it was hypothetically impossible without this.) NOT ~~I can't have passed~~ ...
*"I should have invited her." "Don't worry, she **couldn't have come** anyway."* (= In the hypothetical situation in which she was invited, it was impossible for her.) NOT ~~She can't have come~~ ...

▶ **07.10** **Other expressions**

*We **are bound to** find a cure for cancer one day.* (= certain speculation)
*You **can tell** (**that**) John is intelligent from the books he reads.* (= certain deduction)
*In the future, it**'s (highly) likely** (**that**) cars will be electric.* (= likely)
***I bet* / *I reckon* / *I'm quite sure* (that)** most movies will be in 3D.* (= likely)
***There's a/an outside/slim/good chance* (that)** I'll be the only applicant.*
***There's no way* / *It's highly unlikely* (that)** there is life on Mars.*

I must have pressed the wrong button.

a Choose the best option.

1 Don't worry, we *might* / *will* / *can* arrive in plenty of time.
2 The two teams are equally matched, and it *'s going to* / *may* / *can* be a great game.
3 It's *highly* / *absolutely* / *completely* unlikely that government policy will change.
4 Food prices *should* / *must* / *could* get out of control.
5 I'm sure Andrew *could* / *can* / *will* have realized that it was only a joke.
6 There's a *slim* / *narrow* / *minor* chance that they will change their mind.
7 In fact, you *must* / *can* / *should* find people who live on less than a dollar a day.
8 Someone *must* / *can* / *should* have leaked the news; it's all over the Internet.
9 We *must not* / *needn't* / *can't* have run out of milk. I got some this morning.
10 You *can* / *must* / *should* tell they get along. They're always laughing and joking.

b Rewrite these sentences using the words in parentheses.

1 It was impossible for Adam to do any more. (couldn't)
  Adam couldn't have done any more.
2 I'm sure that customers will complain. (bound)
3 It is very possible that I'll see Ian tomorrow. (well)
4 I think Barbara broke the window; she was playing around here. (must)
5 There's no way the referee saw the incident. (can't)
6 Damien probably knows the answer. (should)
7 It's obvious to me that Greta is dissatisfied. (tell)
8 The lights are on, so Karen will be at home. (got)

c Check (✓) the words 1–10 in *italics* that are possible. Correct the mistakes you find.

  Could
[1] ~~May~~ time travel become a reality? Scientists have been contemplating the idea for centuries, and in movies like *Back to the Future* and *Predestination* we [2]*might* get the idea that time travel is a real possibility. In many ways, this is wishful thinking; it [3]*will* be amazing to go back to ancient Egypt and see the pyramids being built. Unfortunately, there's [4]*not way* that time travel is possible at our current stage of technological development. Maybe if we [5]*could* travel close to, even beyond, the speed of light, new horizons [6]*might* open up, but that is a distant possibility. Still, if we [7]*can* build a machine to approach the speed of light, the laws of physics would change and we [8]*must* enter new territory. This all sounds [9]*as fantasy* and, sadly for science fiction fans, it is until we make some incredible breakthroughs. Time travel [10]*can't* be happening anytime soon, but we can dream and watch the movies, of course.

d ≫ Now go back to p. 81.

7B Cleft sentences

We use cleft sentences to correct, emphasize, or point out <u>information</u>. We form **a focusing phrase ending in *be*** at the beginning of the sentence.

▶ 07.16 ***Wh-* cleft sentences**
Reading other people's comments online bores me.
What bores me is <u>reading other people's comments online</u>.

What	noun	verb phrase	*be*	information focused on
What	*she*	*suggested*	*was*	*out of the question.*
What		*went wrong*	*was*	*that Sheila got involved.*
What		*is amazing*	*is*	*that nobody found out.*

> ### 💡 Tip
> - *be* can be plural if what follows it is plural:
>   *What patients demand **is/are** better hospitals.*
> - In informal speech we can also use *where/when/why/how* in the *Wh-* cleft structure:
>   ***Where I was born is*** *Shanghai.*
>   ***How I feel is*** *angry.*
>   ***Why I left was*** *to get a job.*

We frequently emphasize an action or activity with *What +happen + be + (that) +* clause:
What happened was that *we had to throw all the food away.*
What happens is that *you get a quick orientation on your first day.*
We can emphasize actions with *What +* noun phrase *+ do + be +(to) +* base form:
What she did was <u>(to) phone the police</u>.
What Sheila had wanted was <u>to get married</u>.

- ***All***
  We can begin cleft sentences with *all*:
  All (that) she wants is *a new phone.*
  All I did was *ask her how she was feeling.*

- ***The thing / One thing*, etc.**
  We can begin cleft sentences with *the first thing, the main thing*, etc.
  The main thing is *that you two stop arguing.*
  One thing you can do is *to promise it won't happen again.*

- ***The place where / time when / reason why***
  We use *place where, time when,* and *reason why* to emphasize a place, time, or reason. We can use *that* instead of *where, when,* and *why*:
  The place* (*where*) *I was born is *Miami.*
  The time* (*when*) *you find out who your real friends are is *when you have no money.*
  The only reason* (*why*) *I stay in this job is *Mike.*
  The main reason* (*why*) *I do it is *to make a little money.*

▶ 07.17 ***It* cleft sentences**
Cathy had the idea.
It was <u>Cathy</u> *who had the idea.*

It	*be*	information focused on (noun/place/time phrase)	that / which / when clause
It	*is*	*technology*	*that is causing increased shyness.*
It	*was*	*the weekend already*	*when she got back to me.*
It	*is*	*working all day for nothing*	*which gets me down.*
It	*is*	*only in big cities*	*that smog is a problem.*

We can also emphasize time with *It is/was not until … that* and *It is/was only when … that*:
It was not until *Lesley went away* **that** *I realized how much I missed her.*
It's only when *I'm alone* **that** *I feel insecure.*

What technology does is to bring people together.

a Match the sentence halves.

1	*e* What he wanted was	a	write an angry letter back.
2	☐ What I did was	b	that the problems start.
3	☐ It was my teacher	c	that the boat started to sink.
4	☐ All you can do is	d	who encouraged me to write.
5	☐ It's only when we're busy	e	to change the world.
6	☐ What happened was	f	try harder next time.

b Correct the mistakes in the sentences.
1 ~~There~~ It is Paris that I've always wanted to visit.
2 The captain of the ship was she who sensed the storm coming.
3 All what students want is an affordable educational system.
4 All she did was taking out the cable.
5 What happens next is to fill out an application form.
6 The most important thing is which he is innocent.
7 What was the weather that was beginning to worry me.
8 Is a unique situation that we find ourselves in.

c Rewrite the sentences as cleft sentences using the words in parentheses.
1 I want coffee. (what) *What I want is coffee.*
2 I only need ten dollars. (all)
3 Nobody wants to do this job. (it)
4 You are asking for something unreasonable. (what)
5 We chose Portugal because of the friendly people. (reason)
6 Our car ran into a tree. (happened)
7 Her cousin was causing all the trouble. (it)
8 I don't know Jason so well and this bothers me. (the thing)

d ⟫ Now go back to p. 83.

Gerunds

Gerunds are -*ing* forms that function as nouns in a sentence. The whole clause becomes a gerund when we add -*ing* to the verb:

sleep too much → *Sleeping too much* is as bad as *sleeping too little*.

We can form compound nouns with gerunds:
sleeping pills, *on-the-job training*

Gerunds are much more common than infinitives as subjects:
Staying in bed all day is not a great use of your time.
To stay in bed all day is ... = unusual

We use gerunds after prepositions and certain expressions, such as *it's (not) worth, it's no good/use, there's no point (in)*:

*I am interested **in becoming** a member of your club.*
NOT *~~in to become~~*
*Do you ever get tired **of Jill getting home** late every night?*
NOT *~~of Jill to get~~*
Was it worth spending all that money on a sofa bed?
There's no point worrying and losing sleep over it.

Infinitives

We use the base form (infinitive without *to*) after modal verbs, expressions like *had better, would rather,* some verbs like *let* and *make*, and as imperatives:
*The situation may well **get** worse before it gets better.*
*I would rather **sleep** in my own bed than in a hotel room.*
*Be quiet! Let me **have** some sleep tonight.*

We use an infinitive after ...

- many adjectives, comparatives, superlatives, and ordinal numbers:
  *I was **delighted to hear** that you had won first prize.* NOT *~~delighted hearing~~*
  *Who is the **greatest** athlete ever **to represent** the United States?* NOT *~~representing~~*
  *She was the **first** woman **to climb** Everest.* NOT *~~climbing~~*
- nouns formed from verbs that take the infinitive, e.g., *agreement, decision, plan* but NOT *expectation* or *hope*, which take *of* + gerund:
  *Sally made a **decision to resign**.*
  *I had **hopes of getting** on the team.* NOT *~~hopes to get~~*
  For verb patterns with gerunds and infinitives see p. 176.
- time
  *It's **time to go** to bed.*
  *There's still **time to register** for the competition.*
- quantifiers like *enough, little,* and *many* + nouns
  *Do you have **enough** money **to start** your own business?*
  *I've seen **too many** movies like that **to be** very impressed.*

▶ 08.02

	Active gerunds	Passive gerunds
Present	***Shouting** a lot isn't very good for your voice.* *I can't stand **not knowing** what I'm supposed to do.*	*Winning is better than **being beaten**.* *What I resent is **not being given** the opportunity to show what I can do.*
Perfect	*I'm sorry for ever **having mentioned** the subject.* *I regret **not having contacted** you earlier.*	*The star denied **having been seen** with the actor.* *The worst thing is **not having been told**.*

▶ 08.03

	Active infinitives	Passive infinitives
Simple	*I'll **come**.* *Try **to help**, if you can.*	*Don't **be put off** by the noise.* *This offer is **not to be missed**.*
Continuous	*I'd rather **be going** with you.* *She seems **to be feeling** better.*	*It should **be being done** as we speak.* *The space seems **to be being used** as a parking lot.* (unusual)
Perfect	*You'd better **have finished** by the time I get back.* *It's important **to have tried**.*	*Louise must not **have been treated** very well.* *I wouldn't like **to have been given** that job.*
Perfect continuous	*We will **have been seeing** each other for two years in April.* *I'm proud **to have been working** here for so many years.*	*Joe must **have been being bullied** at school.* (unusual)

> 💡 **Tip**
> Perfect forms of gerunds and infinitives stress that the activity is in the past and complete. We can often use present forms with exactly the same meaning:
> *Her proudest moment to date is **having won** / **winning** Olympic gold.*
> *I wasn't happy at **having been compared** / **being compared** to someone 20 years older.*
> *You were supposed **to have finished** / **to finish** it yesterday.*

> 💡 **Tip**
> Some adjectives, e.g., *afraid, sorry, sure*, are followed by the gerund or infinitive with a difference in meaning:
> *I'm **sure to see** Tom at work on Monday.*
> *sure* = focus on probability of something happening
> *I'm **sure seeing** Tom again will be amazing.*
> *sure* = focus on emotion / effect of something happening

---

a Choose the correct option.

1 *Choosing* / *Having chosen* / *To be chosen* a pillow that is right for your back is not easy.
2 *Picking* / *Being picked* / *Having been picked* for my college team would be a great achievement.
3 There was no point *waiting* / *having been waited* / *to wait* for him.
4 Jane is furious with me for *mislead* / *having misled* / *having been misled* her.
5 The suspect claims *to have been visiting* / *to be visiting* / *to have been visited* her sister at that time.
6 I would prefer *not to have known* / *to have known not*.
7 Sorry, but there are too few players *to have* / *having* a real game.
8 There's no use *having complained* / *complaining* / *to complain* about it all the time.
9 Look, it's time *to forget* / *forgetting* everything that happened.
10 The views from the top are worth *describing* / *to be described* in detail.

b Correct the mistakes in the gerunds and infinitives in *italics*.

Is it possible for someone never [1]*~~to be sleeping~~* (to sleep)? The answer is (almost) yes if you have Fatal Familial Insomnia, in which [2]*to have fallen* asleep is almost impossible. For sufferers, it's not even worth them [3]*to go* to bed because sleep won't come. As the name suggests, [4]*affecting* by this rare but dreadful condition can cause death, depending on its severity. If we don't get enough sleep [5]*carry out* our day-to-day life, the damage to our physical and mental health can be very serious. [6]*To not sleep* for days often makes people [7]*to feel* weak and disoriented. There can be some benefit in [8]*being taken* sleeping pills, but this puts a different kind of stress on the body, and the drugs can become addictive. There is a need for more research [9]*doing* in this area, and it is sure [10]*being* a very deserving way for government money [11]*to be spending*.

c ≫ Now go back to p. 93.

8B Conditionals

We often refer to conditionals as real, unreal, and mixed. These are useful reference points for verb forms, but there are many variations with different tenses and conjunctions.

▶ 08.09 **Real and unreal conditionals**

In real conditionals there is no change of use of verb forms. We use present tenses in the *if* clause:

Present Real *If I **want** a snack, I **have** one.*
Future Real *She**'ll recover** quickly if her temperature **goes** down.*

In unreal conditionals we show that a situation is hypothetical or unlikely by changing the verb forms back one tense:

Present and Future Unreal *If it **weren't raining**, I **would go** out somewhere. (It is raining now.)*
*If it **was/were*** my choice, we'd go to the spa.*
**We can use* If ... was *or* If ... were.

Past Unreal *Megan **wouldn't have missed** her plane if she **hadn't lost** her passport. (She lost her passport.)*
*The car **could have gone** off the road if he **had been driving** any faster.*

Mixed *I **would speak** French more fluently **if I had been allowed** to study in France.*
*If I **knew** what you wanted, I**'d have done** it a long time ago.*

> 🔍 **Tip**
> We can put *had, should,* and *were* first instead of *if*. This is formal.
> **Had I known** about your plans earlier, I would have acted differently.
> **Should her condition get worse**, we will contact you immediately.
> **Were humans to live** so long, there would be many health complications.

▶ 08.10 **Other conjunctions**

as long as / so long as / on the condition that = only if **in the event of + noun** (formal)	You can borrow my shirt **so long as** you don't get it dirty. Goods can be returned **on the condition that** you have the original receipt. Assemble outside the school **in the event of** a fire.
if + it + be + not for + noun phrase **but for + noun phrase** (formal)	**If it were not for** Simon, I would never have known about the cucumber diet. The negotiations would have failed **but for** my efforts.
providing / provided that = if	The material will be ready **providing that** you give plenty of notice. **Provided that** you repay it within three months, the bank will issue the loan.
suppose / imagine (that)	**Suppose** we could live to 100; what would we look like? **Imagine** there were no school today. Wouldn't that be great?
assuming / supposing = this might be the case	Let's meet on Sunday, **assuming** that is everyone's day off. **Supposing** you could find the treasure, what would you do with it?
(just) in case + possible situation or result = as a precaution **in case of + noun** (formal)	Write down the phone number **just in case** you forget it. **In case of** emergency, call this number.
otherwise + possible result = if not that, then this	I need to get to bed, **otherwise** I won't be able to get up on time. I didn't see her, **otherwise** I would have told her.

a Match the sentence halves.

1 [j] If Sandra gets here early,
2 [ ] If she had said that to me,
3 [ ] If I'm still working in an hour,
4 [ ] If you had bothered to ask,
5 [ ] If the story were to get out,
6 [ ] I don't mind going to the party
7 [ ] I'm happy to share,
8 [ ] If it hadn't been for night school,
9 [ ] I'd better get on with my work
10 [ ] Figure it out yourselves,

a I could have explained everything.
b in case the boss is here today.
c I'd be absolutely furious.
d provided that I can choose first.
e otherwise I'll have to get involved.
f stop me and tell me to go to bed.
g I would never have met my wife.
h it wouldn't look very good for the firm.
i as long as it doesn't finish too late.
j let her in for me, please.

b Put the conditional sentences in order, adding commas where necessary. The first word is highlighted.

1 this / you / hard / if / think / wait / is / just
If you think this is hard, just wait.
2 you / I / with / if / I / were / a / have / would / her / word
3 you / quiet / stay / as / can / you / keep / long / as
4 anyone / me / to / if / is / blame / it's
5 disappointed / Sheila / have / come / been / would / had / if / nobody
6 is / agree / that / on / this / only / will / the / confidential / condition / I / kept
7 to / you / I / find / will / the / be / out / know / should / first
8 assuming / we / everything / need / it / take / won't / long / have / we

c ⟫ Now go back to p. 96.

▶ 09.04 **Reflexive pronouns**

We use reflexive pronouns …

- when the object is the same as the subject:
  *They blamed **themselves** for the accident.*
  *She's always looking at **herself** in the mirror.*
- after verbs and prepositions:
  *The director of the bank awarded **himself** a big bonus.*
  *Don't be angry with **yourself**.*
  *I said to **myself** that I would try again the next day.*
- after nouns and pronouns to emphasize importance, and for contrast with other people/things in general:
  *The president **himself** has shares in the company.*
  *The boss **herself** does not believe any of these rumors.*
- after the verb phrase to emphasize independence/achievement:
  *We designed the house **ourselves**.*
  *They cleaned up the city **themselves**.*
- after the verb phrase to show similarity to another person/thing = *as well*
  *He went to take a shower. I needed one **myself**.*

Cars that park **themselves** do save a lot of space.

We use *by* + reflexive pronoun to mean without anybody else:
*My friends were busy, so I went into town **by myself**.*
We use *beside* + reflexive pronoun to mean worried/upset:
*After the last heavy defeat, the manager is **beside himself**.*
Some verbs have a different meaning when the object is a reflexive pronoun:
*He didn't **behave himself**.* = behave well
*Just **be yourself** in the interview.* = act naturally
*You don't want to **find yourself** alone.* = get into a situation
*I **helped myself** to the sandwiches.* = take without invitation
*I **didn't feel myself**.* = feel different from usual
Verbs that are usually done by an individual, for example *shave*, *wash*, etc., don't need a reflexive pronoun, unless we want to make a point of the ability:
I washed and dressed in five minutes.
*The twins are old enough to dress **themselves**.*
In English we do not generally use the verbs *concentrate, feel, hurry, lie* (*down*), *relax, sit* (*down*) with reflexive pronouns:
Rebecca didn't feel comfortable living in such a huge city.
NOT ~~feel herself~~
I spent some time relaxing before the busy day ahead.
NOT ~~relaxing myself~~
I concentrated on my work. NOT ~~concentrated myself~~

▶ 09.05 **Reciprocal pronouns**

We use *each other* and *one another* with plural subjects:
*We always speak to **each other** with the utmost respect.*
One another is more formal than *each other*. It is often used when more than two people are involved:
*We chatted with **each other**.*
*They greeted **one another** before addressing the room.*
Compare reflexive and reciprocal pronouns:
*Mr. and Mrs. Smith bought **themselves** a car.* (one car for them both)
*Mr. and Mrs. Smith bought **each other** a present.* (two presents, one each)
*We smiled at **each other** and said hello.*
*We smiled to **ourselves** but gave no sign of any emotion.*
We use the possessives *each other's* and *one another's*:
*They were friends and regular visitors at **each other's** houses.*
*The purpose of this session is to listen to **one another's** problems sympathetically.*

---

a Match a and b in each pair with the best endings.

1 a ☐ We looked at ourselves   1 and smiled.
   b ☐ We looked at each other   2 in the mirror.

2 a ☐ They usually behave themselves   1 when the teacher's around.
   b ☐ They usually behave   2 better when the teacher's around.

3 a ☐ Mike helped him   1 clean up the room.
   b ☐ Mike helped himself   2 to a slice of cake.

4 a ☐ He looked really upset, so I sat down   1 beside himself.
     2 beside him.
   b ☐ He looked really upset. He was

5 a ☐ They found themselves   1 after searching for hours.
   b ☐ They finally found each other   2 in a very awkward situation.

6 a ☐ The three medalists shook hands to   1 congratulate themselves on their success.
   b ☐ Atlético Madrid can   2 congratulate each other on their success.

b Choose the correct option.

1 I think we'll treat *us / ourselves* to a nice box of chocolates.
2 *John himself / Himself* would never have thought of that.
3 Laura only thinks of *each other / herself*. She's so selfish.
4 "Can I borrow a pen?" "Sorry, I don't have one *myself / itself*."
5 You don't need to help. I can do the puzzle *itself / myself*.
6 Dom can't imagine *by himself / himself* in a different job.
7 They kissed *one another / themselves* and said goodbye.
8 The students checked *each other's / each others'* answers.

c Add the missing reflexive and reciprocal pronouns.

Have you ever thought to ask ^yourself^ whether you would like to live in space? As the world population grows, towns and cities find under tremendous pressure, and it is becoming more difficult and expensive for us just to live in urban areas, let alone enjoy there. So maybe we would feel more comfortable in space. But, let's just remind of the challenges of doing such a thing. The technology may be there, but we would be opening up to lots of problems we can't even imagine. Unfortunately, there are no easy solutions. The world needs to sort out, and we need to learn to live with. I hope I've made clear.

d ⋙ Now go to p. 106.

9B Ellipsis and substitution

We can avoid repeating our own or other people's ideas using ellipsis (leaving out words and phrases) and substitution (replacing words and phrases).

▶ **09.11** **Leaving out subjects, main verbs, and auxiliaries**

We can leave out repeated subjects, main verbs, and auxiliaries after *and/or/but/then* when the subject is the same:
The planning commission has spent a lot of money, but (it has) *changed nothing.*
The architect designed an iconic office tower, then (the architect designed) *a bridge.*
We usually can't leave out subjects and auxiliaries in clauses connected with words like *although/because/before/if/when*, etc.:
You can't comment because you have no appreciation of art.
NOT ~~because have~~
I changed my mind when I saw the building. NOT ~~when saw~~

▶ **09.12** **Leaving out verb phrases**

We can leave out repeated verb phrases and use an auxiliary or modal instead. The auxiliary or modal may change in the second verb:
The city council promised to **build a new playground,** *but it never* **did.**
Graham said he would **show you how to do it** *and he* **will.**
We shorten the infinitive to *to* but don't leave it out completely:
I needed to go shopping, but the kids didn't want to (go shopping).
NOT ~~didn't want~~
I haven't seen the exhibition, but I ought to (see it). NOT ~~ought~~

▶ **09.13** **Other examples of ellipsis**

We can leave out adjectives and repeat *be*:
I'm quite comfortable here. **Are** *you* (quite comfortable)?
The first room **was** *beautiful, but the second* **wasn't** (beautiful).
We can leave out noun phrases after determiners and superlatives:
This is **my** *favorite picture, and that's* **my husband's** (favorite picture).
There were a few apartments in my price range, and I chose the cheapest (apartment in my price range).
We can leave out repeated verbs and nouns in comparative structures:
They built the first floor quicker than (they built) *the second* (floor).
The Park is the most expensive hotel, and The Seaview (is) *the second* (most expensive hotel).

▶ **09.14** ***so / neither / nor***

We use *so/neither* + auxiliary/*be* + subject to avoid repeating exactly the same idea for a new subject:
The old town is amazing, and **so** *are the views.* = the views are also amazing
If Gerald doesn't like it, **neither/nor** *will his wife.* = his wife also won't like it
nor can also mean *and not*:
She doesn't want to live in the country **nor** *in the town.* = and she doesn't want to live in the town

▶ **09.15** ***so* and *not***

We can use *so* and *not* instead of clauses after verbs like *believe, guess, imagine, be afraid, appear, assume, seem, hope, presume, suspect,* and *say*:
We don't know if the diamond is real, but we think **so.**
I suspect **not** *but I'm not sure, so ask someone else.*
We use a negative verb + *so* with verbs like *believe, expect, imagine,* and *think*:
I thought it would be a good game, but I don't think **so** *now.*
We can use *if not* and *if so* instead of clauses:
I hope you finish that report. **If not,** *give it to me anyway.*
Some of you look confused. **If so,** *see me after and I'll explain again.*

▶ **09.16** **Pronouns**

We can use pronouns like *one* and *ones* to substitute noun phrases:
There are ten different colors to choose from. Which **ones** *do you want?*
We can use *that* instead of a phrase or clause:
Don't interrupt me! I hate **that.**
We can use possessive pronouns, *yours, mine,* etc., to substitute noun phrases:
You've got a decent view, but **mine** *is terrible.*
You know my views on private education, so tell me **yours.**

---

a Cross out the words that can be left out of each sentence with no change of meaning.

1 The president arrived and he made a speech.
2 You don't know and you never will know.
3 I will tell you because I value and I respect your opinion.
4 We have been thinking about our reputation, we have not been thinking about money.
5 I said I would be volunteering, so I will be volunteering.
6 If they are hungry, bears can be dangerous and they can be unpredictable.
7 My first impression was very positive, but my second wasn't very positive.
8 We can meet up at seven if you'd like to meet up tonight.
9 "Are we in room six?" "I guess we are not in room six."
10 The Nile is the longest river in the world, and the Amazon is the second longest river in the world.

b Shorten the sentences using substitution.

1 My exam was a lot tougher than ~~your exam~~. *(yours)*
2 "Is this the right page?" "I think it is the right page."
3 "I don't know where we are." "I don't know where we are, either."
4 I love vacations abroad, especially long vacations abroad.
5 "Who has a dress with short sleeves?" "Borrow my dress with short sleeves."
6 "Did you get my message?" "I'm afraid we didn't get it."
7 "George got married." "I didn't know George had gotten married."
8 Klaus is very enthusiastic and his sister is very enthusiastic, too.
9 Tina had always wanted to go parachuting, and one day she went parachuting.

c Use ellipsis and substitution to shorten the conversation and make it more natural.

Damien I've been thinking about the office of the future.
Rachel What do you mean by ~~the office of the future~~? *that*
D The place where we are going to work and where we are going to do business, say, 50 years from now. Those offices will look completely different compared to the offices today.
R I expect they will look completely different.
D For example, imagine there are no walls and there are no doors. All barriers to communication will be broken down and all barriers to communication will be a thing of the past. This is hard to imagine, but you don't need to imagine it. Just go to any successful company today.
R I think successful companies today have walls and have doors.
D You are being sarcastic and you are trying to make fun of me.
R Sorry, I didn't mean to make fun of you. I'd like to travel in time and I'd like to visit an office of the future. Tell me when you have built an office of the future.

d ≫ **Communication 9B** Work in pairs. Student A go to p. 135. Student B go to p. 136.

▶ 10.06 Conditionals

We can use unreal conditionals for (self-)criticism and regret.
Using hypothetical forms to provide critical suggestions can soften your suggestions:

*You**'d get** a better response **if** you **toned** down your language.*
*I **wouldn't have come if** you**'d told** me you weren't interested.*
*If you**'d been watching** properly, you**'d be able to do** it!*
*If I**'d realized** my boss was going to be there, I **would never have said** that.*
*If you **told** a few jokes, the audience **might listen**.*

▶ 10.07 Modals

We use modal + *have* + past participle for (self-)criticism and regret:

could	I **could have timed** my talk better.	= It was desirable but didn't happen.
might	You **might have told** me he was going to be in the audience.	
should	You **should have asked** me first.	= It was the right thing to do, but it didn't happen.
ought to	We **ought to have checked** the equipment.	
shouldn't	He **shouldn't have taken** the car.	= It was the wrong thing to do, but it happened.

> **Tip** We can use *must* for criticism but not *must have*:
> *You **must** listen more carefully in future!*
> *You should have listened more carefully.* NOT ~~must have listened~~
> Use the phrase *You shouldn't have* to show you are grateful for something:
> *Wow, flowers! **You shouldn't have.***

▶ 10.08 would like / love / hate / rather / prefer

We use *would like / love / prefer* + perfect infinitive to talk about regrets:
*I **would love to have spent** more time with you.*
We can use *would hate / not like* + perfect infinitive to sympathize:
*I **would hate to have seen** something like that.*
We use *would (much) rather* with a base form or past tense:
*I **would much rather** see my usual doctor **than** one I don't know.*
*I **would rather** you **didn't do** that in the future.*

▶ 10.09 wish and if only

We use *wish* + simple past for things that we want to change now or in the future:
*I **wish** I **looked** like Jennifer Lawrence.*
*My dad **wishes** he **could** speak Spanish.*
We use *wish* + past perfect for regrets:
*I **wish** I **had met** you ten years ago.*
We use *wish* + person + *would* for criticism:
*I **wish** you **would** switch off that cell phone!*
We use *if only* as a stronger form of *wish*:
*If only Trevor **were** more understanding!*

▶ 10.10 It's time

We can use *it's (about/ high) time* + past tense for criticism:
It's time you got a regular job.
It's about time they came to repair the washing machine.
It's high time she came to her senses and realized nobody is perfect!

---

a Match the sentence halves in each pair.

1 a ☐ We could have gotten home
  b ☐ We could get home

1 provided the trains are running.
2 if the trains had still been running.

2 a ☐ I think if I had been in your shoes
  b ☐ If I were you

1 I'd forget all about it.
2 I would have forgotten all about it by now.

3 a ☐ You couldn't
  b ☐ You shouldn't

1 have done a worse job.
2 have reminded me.

4 a ☐ I wish you would listen to me;
  b ☐ I wish you had listened to me;

1 I have something important to tell you.
2 things might have turned out better.

Anyway, it's time I came to my conclusions.

b Choose the correct option.

1 Julie *couldn't* / *may not* have done it if I hadn't helped her.
2 If you *hadn't dropped* / *didn't drop* the ball, we would have won the game.
3 Staff *ought to* / *shouldn't* complain in front of the customers.
4 I *could* / *would* prefer not to be involved.
5 Jill *should be waiting* / *should have waited* until I got out.
6 You *might* / *should* have passed if you'd studied harder.
7 I'd much rather *hear* / *have heard* the news from you, but it's too late now.
8 We *hope* / *wish* you would reconsider.
9 Oh, I wish I *can* / *could* be there with you next weekend.
10 This bedroom is a mess! It's time you *clean* / *cleaned* it up.

c Fill in each blank with one word.

Michelle Hi, so how did the driving test go?
Ben It was a nightmare! I wish I ¹ _could_ start all over again. If I ² _____ known it would be that bad, I would have stayed in bed.
M What went wrong?
B What went right? I'd ³ _____ not talk about it.
M Oh, go on. What did the examiner say?
B Oh, the usual stuff – "You ⁴ _____ to have used your mirrors more, you ⁵ _____ n't have stopped so quickly. If I ⁶ _____ you, I'd slow down now …" Do you get the idea?
M Well, I suppose you ⁷ _____ have had more lessons.
B If ⁸ _____ I had had the time and the money.
M Maybe it's ⁹ _____ you realized how important it is for you to get a driver's license.
B Oh no, now you're criticizing me!

d ≫ Now go back to p. 118.

10B Passive reporting verbs

We use passive reporting verbs when we are generalizing about what most people say or think:
*The color white **is known** to represent purity in many cultures.*
We also use passive reporting verbs to report information from other sources. They are most common in …
- academic writing where we want to appear objective:
*It **has been shown** (Smith, 2012) that superstition influences behavior.*
- news, either to keep the source secret or because the source is unimportant:
*It **is being reported** that the suspect escaped in a car.*

It + passive + *that* clause
We can use *it* + passive reporting verb + *that* clause with verbs like *know, believe, say, report,* etc.:
*It is widely **known that** the middle of the month was unlucky for the Romans.*
*In ancient times, **it was believed that** the sun went around the Earth.*

Subject + passive + infinitive
We can use passive + infinitive with verbs like *understand* and *think*:
*He **is understood** to be furious.*
*It is **thought to be** good luck to catch falling leaves in the autumn.*
We can follow this structure with perfect infinitives to refer to the past, or continuous infinitives for the present and future:
*She**'s said to have met** him on set.*
*He**'s reported to be working** with DeNiro again.*

It + passive + *wh-* clause
We use passive reporting verbs + clauses beginning with *wh-* words for unknown facts:
*It **is not known what** was said in the meeting.*
*It **was not made clear whether** or not they would be challenging the decision.*
The *wh-* clause can go first in the sentence:
***What was said** in the meeting is not known.*

▶ **10.16**

It + passive + *that* clause only: *announce argue imply note explain suggest*

*It was **announced** that changes would be made. NOT ~~were announced to be made~~*
*It is **argued** that Cleopatra was one of the most influential women in history.*
*In the report it is **implied** that corruption was involved.*
*It should **be noted** that he gave half of his winnings to charity.*
*It was **explained** that the mysterious marks were, in fact, animal tracks.*
*It has not been **suggested** that any jobs will be affected.*

Subject + passive + infinitive only: *consider repute*

*Brian was **considered** to be one of their best players. NOT ~~It is considered that Brian~~ …*
*They are **reputed** to have made millions from the sale of their company.*

Both structures: *acknowledge agree allege assume believe claim expect know report reveal suspect rumor say show think understand*

*It is **alleged** that five men in masks carried out the attack.*
*The ship **isn't expected to be arriving** anytime soon.*
*She **is reported to have made** over ten million dollars.*
*It **is said** that K2 is harder to climb than Everest.*
*The story **has been shown to be** a complete lie.*
*Latin **is thought to have been** the first international language.*

Subject + passive + *as* + adjective/noun phrase: *regarded* seen**

*Serena Williams **is regarded as** one of the greatest tennis players ever. NOT ~~It is regarded that Serena~~*
*Sending cards on special occasions **may be seen as** old-fashioned by some.*

* *regarded/seen + to be* is possible but far less common.

*Walking under a ladder **is believed to be** unlucky!*

a Choose the correct option.

1 An old manuscript is said *to have / that it has* been found by a couple moving into the house.
2 *It / The news* is believed that it happened many years earlier.
3 In the letter it was implied *that Sam / Sam to have* released the data unknowingly.
4 Detectives *were revealed / revealed* that they still had no clues to work on.
5 Once she *was regarded / regarded* as one of the best painters of her generation.
6 It is to be expected *mistakes to be made / that mistakes will be made*.
7 Television has *been shown to / showed that* influence public opinion.

b Correct the mistakes in the sentences.

1 It ^is̶ argued that Vancouver is the most diverse city in the world.
2 He is said that he lived in a cave.
3 It is seen that basketball is very popular in Asia.
4 It was not reported her reply was.
5 It is suspected to the people responsible have left the country.
6 The winters are thought that they get very cold in this part of the world.

c Complete the text with the past participle of a verb in the box.

consider   expect   explain   imply   know   not understand
see   ~~think~~

There is significant cultural variation today, but it is ¹___thought___ that one of the most common, yet oldest, customs is shaking hands. From vases and other archaeological evidence, the ancient Greeks are ²_____ to have shaken hands, and the custom was ³_____ as a sign of respect and affection. In fact, the handshake is ⁴_____ to be a form of ritual because it is done in so many contexts with great attention to detail. For example, in Eastern Europe it is ⁵_____ that a man's, but not a woman's, hand will be shaken every time you meet. In China, by holding on to someone's hand for a short time after a handshake, it is ⁶_____ that you are showing extra respect. It is ⁷_____ how the custom originated, but in some books it is ⁸_____ that by offering your hand without a weapon you come in peace.

d ⟫ Now go to p. 121.

This page is intentionally left blank.

6A Adjectives: Describing images

a ▶️ 06.01 Complete the sentences below with the adjectives in the box. Listen and check. Sometimes more than one answer is possible.

playful	exotic
powerful	iconic
humorous	gritty
raw	evocative
meaningful	ironic
well-composed	nonsensical

1 The strength of emotion in this close-up of her face seemed to almost hit me. It's a truly _____ image.

2 He appears to be lifting a car with one hand. It's just not possible – it's completely _____.

3 The kittens are loving that ball of wool! It's an extremely _____ photo.

4 The photographer has captured _____ scenes of inner-city poverty. It isn't pretty.

5 It's a very _____ photo. There's a perfect balance between the foreground and the sky and the land.

6 These photos make a more _____ statement about man's impact on the environment than words could.

7 This is the most gently _____ photo in his portfolio. The expression on the man's face really makes me smile.

8 For me, the most wonderfully _____ photo in the exhibition is the frozen desert. It's another world for me.

9 It's a very _____ image. You can't look at it without feeling something.

10 This photo was taken just after he lost the game. The _____ emotion is painful to look at.

11 The picture of Neil Armstrong stepping on to the moon in 1969 is truly _____.

12 The rather _____ expression on the woman's face seems to be saying, Oh, well, life's like that.

b Notice the suffix in these adjectives:
- play**ful**
- power**ful**
- meaning**ful**

Underline more adjective suffixes in **a**. Which adjective doesn't have a suffix? Think of two more adjectives which have each suffix you underlined.

c ▶️ 06.02 Match sentences 1–6 with a–f. Listen and check.

1 ☐ The angle of this photo shows off the iconic architecture of the new art gallery.

2 ☐ In this powerful photo, the house stands alone against its environment.

3 ☐ I like this photo of the room where everything is neatly arranged.

4 ☐ In this photo, he's wearing an exotic costume with feathers and gold ribbons.

5 ☐ All the pictures in the exhibition are virtually the same.

6 ☐ You need the perfect flower and the perfect light.

a It's not too **cluttered**.
b It looks **sensational**.
c It's quite a **bleak** image.
d It gets a little **repetitive**.
e If these elements are right, you can create an absolutely **flawless** image.
f It all looks very **elaborate**.

> 💡 **Tip**
>
> Many adverbs of degree and adjectives form very strong collocations. For example, we say *utterly miserable* and *incredibly elaborate*, but ~~utterly elaborate~~ isn't a natural collocation. It's a good idea to note adverb + adjective collocations in your vocabulary notebook.

d Underline the adverb of degree + adjective collocations in the sentences in **a**.

e Which of the adverbs of degree in the box can be used with which adjectives in **bold** in **c**?

incredibly	pretty	a little	wonderfully
extremely	utterly	rather	truly

f ≫ Communication 6A Now go to p. 134.

7A Compound adjectives: Parts of the body

> **Tip**
> Compound adjectives are formed in many ways:
> - noun + adjective: ***world-famous, self-confident***
> - adjective + noun + -ed: ***short-sleeved, cold-blooded***
> - adjective + participle: ***good-looking, long-running***
> - adverb + participle: ***hard-working, well-written***
> - noun + participle: ***heartbreaking, self-made***
>
> Unless they have become one word, e.g., *heartbreaking*, the forms listed here always require a hyphen (-) between the two parts.

> **Tip**
> Compound adjectives are usually well-established collocations.
> *The novel is **heartbreaking / mind-blowing**.* NOT ~~*The novel is **heart-opening** / **mind-breaking***~~ etc.
>
> Many have idiomatic meanings. For example, if a person is ***tongue-tied***, it does not literally mean that their tongue is tied. It means they find it difficult to speak because they are shy, nervous, or embarrassed.

a ▶ 07.01 Look at examples 1–4 and then complete 5–9. Listen and check.

- **adjective + noun + -ed**
  1 He considers other points of view – he has an open mind. ➔ He's **open-minded**.
  2 She will always help her friends – she has a warm heart. ➔ She's **warm-hearted**.
- **noun + present participle**
  3 Carrying boxes upstairs nearly broke my back.
     ➔ It was **backbreaking** work.
  4 The sight of elderly people in love always warms my heart. ➔ It's a **heartwarming** sight.

  5 She always uses her left hand.
     ➔ She's …

  6 Don't expect any sympathy – he has a very hard heart. ➔ He's …

  7 She made the decision with a clear head.
     ➔ She's …

What we should do is …

  8 Thai food makes my mouth water.
     ➔ It's …

  9 The sight made my jaw drop.
     ➔ The sight was …

b ▶ 07.02 Match the words in the boxes to make compound adjectives that can replace the definitions in *italics*. Use some words more than once. Listen and check.

half near hair	sighted	headed
absent narrow	raising	hearted
light mind	boggling	minded

1 Everyone in the village disapproves of my lifestyle. They're all so *unwilling to accept different ideas*.
2 He agreed to help us move the furniture, but it was very *lacking in enthusiasm*.
3 He may forget to call you. He's rather *likely to forget things because he's thinking about something else*.
4 Can you tell me what that sign says? I'm afraid I'm *unable to see distant things clearly*.
5 After eating nothing for ten hours, I began to feel a little *as if I might lose my balance*.
6 I'm fed up with serious movies. I'd like to see something more *happy and not too serious*.
7 The brakes on the bus weren't working properly, so it was a *terrifying* journey.
8 Did you know there are 100 billion stars just in our own galaxy? It's *almost impossible to imagine*.

c ▶ 07.03 Pronunciation

1 Listen to the two pairs of compound adjectives. <u>Underline</u> the main stress. Is it on the first or the second word?

mind-boggling	open-minded
heartwarming	half-hearted

2 <u>Underline</u> the main stress in these patterns. Practice saying the compound adjectives in **a**.
- adjective + body part + -*ed*
- body part + present participle

d 💬 Find someone in the class who:

1 is left-handed
2 ate something mouthwatering yesterday
3 has done a backbreaking job at some time in their life
4 thinks they're open-minded
5 thinks they're absent-minded
6 has been on a hair-raising journey
7 knows a mind-boggling fact
8 has never felt tongue-tied.

e ≫ Now go back to p. 81.

8B Aging and health

a ▶ 08.07 Listen to the words and phrases in the box.

a glowing complexion   smooth skin   saggy skin
oily skin   dry skin   wrinkles / fine lines   freckles
a rash   blotches   spots/acne   firm skin   clear skin

Which words in the box are usually associated with … ?

- youthful skin
- mature skin
- all ages

b Complete the collocations in **bold** with as many words and phrases as possible from the box in **a**. Compare your ideas with a partner. Are they the same?

1 Sun exposure can **cause** …
2 If you have an allergic reaction, your skin might **break out in** …
3 **Anti-aging creams** are designed to **prevent** …
4 Young people are often **prone to** …
5 Most people hate it when they start **getting** …
6 A **facial** can be helpful if you **have** …
7 If you want to be a model, it helps to **have** …

c ▶ 08.08 Match 1–9 with a–i. Listen and check.

1 ☐ He was **showing his age**. His
2 ☐ Her **eyesight is deteriorating** and
3 ☐ **Yellowing teeth**? Try our new
4 ☐ **Moisturizing** daily combined with **weekly facials**
5 ☐ **Tooth loss** and **heart trouble** are
6 ☐ **Strengthening** and **toning** exercises
7 ☐ **Poor circulation** can be improved by
8 ☐ **Weight loss** can be aided by
9 ☐ There's no need to resort to painful **injections**

a **whitening** toothpaste. You'll be amazed.
b **regular cardiovascular exercise**.
c **eating a varied and balanced diet**.
d helps to **tighten** and **plump** the skin.
e **hair was thinning** and **graying** around the temples.
f like yoga and Pilates help to give you energy.
g or **plastic surgery**.
h not inevitable parts of aging.
i she **has arthritis** in her knees.

d Look at the words and phrases in **bold** in **c**. Complete the chart.

Anti-aging treatments/effects	
Superficial effects of aging	
Health problems caused by aging	
Healthy living	

e 💬 Answer the questions about the things in **d**.

1 What anti-aging techniques do you think are reasonable steps to take to stop the aging process?
2 Do you think that any of the superficial effects of aging can be prevented/cured?
3 Which health problems caused by aging have affected people you know? What happened?
4 Which healthy living technique is the most important? Can you add any more to the chart?

f ⟫ Now go to p. 96.

9B Describing buildings

a Complete the sentences with the adjectives in the box. Sometimes more than one answer is possible.

imposing	nondescript	graceful
innovative	tasteless	over the top
out of place	stunning	dated

1 The planning commission favored an original design by a young architect because they wanted a striking and _____ town hall to bring a modern edge to their city.
2 As the town is fairly small, the large castle on the hill is really too _____ and seems _____.
3 I'm sorry, but there's nothing remarkable or new about the design of those houses – they're totally _____ and pretty _____.
4 I really like the gold leaf in the ceiling decorations, but for some people it's _____ and _____.
5 The _____, elegant lines of the building are very pleasing to the eye. It's _____.

b ▶ 09.10 Match words 1–10 with the pictures below. Listen and check.

1 ☐ cabin
2 ☐ skyscraper
3 ☐ power station
4 ☐ subdivision
5 ☐ warehouse
6 ☐ penthouse
7 ☐ studio
8 ☐ cottage
9 ☐ mansion
10 ☐ strip mall

c Put the words in **b** in these groups.
1 places that can be homes
2 places that are businesses
3 places that can be both

d 💬 Answer the questions.
1 Which residential buildings are common in your country? Which are less common?
2 If you had a lot of money, would you live in a mansion, a penthouse, or neither? Why?
3 If you had to live in a small space, would you prefer a cabin or a studio? Why?

e ⟫ Now go back to p. 107.

10A Communication verbs

a ▶ 10.02 Complete the sentences with the verbs in the box. Listen and check.

address   presented   go into
demonstrated   made
move on to   illustrate

1 She _____ **her understanding** of complex social issues by explaining them in everyday language.
2 I've been invited to _____ **an audience** of business experts at a conference in London.
3 If you sense the audience is getting bored, you should _____ **a new subject** to keep their interest up.
4 Every time she got the wrong slide, she _____ **comments under her breath** that I couldn't hear.
5 She _____ **key information** in easy-to-read charts.
6 It really helps if you can _____ **the points** you want to make with specific examples.
7 Don't _____ **too much detail** during your presentation – people can only process so much new information.

b Match the phrases in **bold** in 1–8 with the definitions a–h.

1 ☐ She began by **paying tribute to** all the teachers who had inspired her throughout her school years.
2 ☐ During the speech, he **asserted** his right to express his opinion even if it wasn't a popular one.
3 ☐ He **backed up** the arguments he made by providing examples from recent research.
4 ☐ She **summarized** the key ideas in her presentation with a list of bullet points.
5 ☐ He saw his speech as an opportunity to **voice concerns about** the rise in crime in his neighborhood.
6 ☐ The leader of the opposition **attacked** government policies in a speech that focused on the rise in unemployment.
7 ☐ In her presentation, she **sold the idea** of more flexible working hours to her managers.
8 ☐ She **concluded** by encouraging more people to try one of their free community education courses.

a to criticize a person or people strongly
b to say the most important facts in a short and clear way
c to publicly praise somebody in front of an audience
d to end a speech or presentation
e to persuade a person or people that something is a good plan
f to publicly say what you think about worrying issues
g to prove that something is true
h to make a statement strongly

c 💬🔊 Think of people you know or in the media who do / have done the things below. Tell a partner about what happened.

1 attack government policy
2 have paid tribute to another person
3 often go into too much detail
4 sometimes make comments under their breath
5 often voice concerns about something
6 sell their ideas well

d 💬🔊 Answer the questions.

1 Have you ever addressed an audience of more than 100 people? If so, how did it feel? If not, how would you feel doing this?
2 If you were giving a presentation, what could you use to illustrate the finer points of a topic to other people?
3 Do you ever make throwaway remarks? If so, do other people take them seriously? If not, why don't you do this?
4 Who's an influential person from your past that you would feel comfortable paying tribute to? What would you say about them?
5 What do you think is a good way to back up your opinion on something?

e ≫ Now go back to p. 116.

10B Superstitions, customs, and beliefs

a ▶ 10.12 Complete the sentences with the words and phrases in the box. Listen and check.

make a wish   traditionally   customary   good fortune
good luck charm   ward off evil

1 She wore a _____ around her neck until the day she died at the ripe old age of 104.
2 I had the _____ to invest at exactly the right time and made millions.
3 The cautionary tales are _____ told by each generation of parents to teach their children morality.
4 It is _____ to decorate the house with branches from pine trees at this time of year.
5 They sprinkle the beans and then sweep every room to banish demons and _____ .
6 Children _____ and try to blow out the candles. It will come true if they manage to blow them all out.

b ▶ 10.13 The words in the box are all used for talking about beliefs. Check (✓) the ones you think you know. Try saying the words. Then listen and check.

gullible	convinced
plausible	convincing
persuasive	far-fetched
dubious	

c Use the words in **b** to replace the definitions below in *italics*. Use a dictionary to help you. There may be more than one possible answer. Which words are very similar in meaning?

1 My friend says a fortune teller's advice led him to success, but I don't find this very *easy to believe*.
2 People who believe in good luck charms must be very *ready to believe anything people tell them*.
3 When she talks about magic, I'm sure what she says is true. She's very *able to make other people believe her*.
4 The idea that horseshoes bring you luck doesn't seem very *likely to be true* to me.
5 I think most things that fortune tellers say are *unlikely to be true*, to say the least.
6 My grandmother was absolutely *certain in her belief* that black cats were unlucky.
7 People's stories about seeing ghosts usually sound rather *difficult to believe* to me.

d Answer the questions.

1 Which of the beliefs in the pictures 1–3 do you find … ?
   • convincing   • plausible   • dubious   • far-fetched
2 As a child, how gullible were you? Can you think of an example?
3 Who do you know (personally or someone well known) who you'd describe as a persuasive person?
4 "People who are convinced they're right are usually wrong." How true do you think this is?

e ⟫ Now go back to p. 119.

If you blow out all your birthday candles with one breath, your wish will come true.

They say that black cats are unlucky.

Some people believe that four-leaf clovers bring good luck.

This page is intentionally left blank.

WRITING FOCUS

Formal letters

Dear Sir/Madam:
I am writing in response to …
I would like to express my (interest in / dissatisfaction with, etc.) …
Please find attached …
I look forward to hearing from you.
Sincerely,

Giving a positive impression

I am very much in touch with …
I enthusiastically maintain my knowledge of …
I played an active role in …
I have been able to …
I have taken a keen interest in …
I feel that, with my … , I would be very well qualified to …

a Look at these extracts from letters. Cross out one word or phrase in each group in *italics* that is less suitable for a formal letter.

1 I *believe / am certain / guess* that my knowledge of local sporting events will enable me to *do / write / contribute* well-informed reviews.
2 I am *writing in response to / answering / replying to* your advertisement, which *was / appeared / was published* in the March issue of your magazine.
3 I look forward to hearing from you *in due time / in a bit / soon*.
4 I'm *an enthusiastic supporter / a real fan / a keen follower* of the local soccer team.
5 *Here are / I am attaching / Please find attached* some sample photos that I took recently.
6 I have *considerable / tons of / extensive* experience of restaurant work.
7 I *am able to be completely flexible / am free any time / can offer a good deal of flexibility* with regard to working hours.
8 I spent some time working on a school magazine and *acquired / developed / picked up* some *relevant / priceless / valuable* editorial skills.

b Add additional formal and positive expressions from **a** to the chart.

c Read the ad and Andy's application email. Rewrite it so that it is in a more formal style.

Dear Sir/Madam:
I am writing …

STAFF NEEDED for a bookstore near the university. Flexible working hours, ideal as a part-time job for students.

To apply, please send an email to:
www.greenstreetbooks.net

job application	🔗 Andy_résumé

Hi there,

Saw your job ad in the student paper and I'd really like to work for you. I'm doing world literature in college, so I know quite a bit about books written by all kinds of people. I'm really into novels and travel books and that'll be useful, won't it? I've never worked in a bookstore before, but I've done café work and I spent a bit of time working in a sporting goods store, so I know all about selling stuff to people. I'm also a nice guy and I've got lots of friends – I can chat with anybody.

So I think I'm just the kind of guy you're looking for. Here's my résumé.

I could work whenever you like, mornings or evenings, it's all the same to me.

Hey, get in touch.

Andy

d ⋙ Now go back to p. 77.

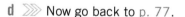 7D Linking: highlighting and giving examples

a Add a transition word or phrase from the chart where there is a ^ in 1–7. Often more than one answer is possible.

1 The team is getting along better now. ^ they have decided to have a team dinner once a month.
2 It is already possible to perceive benefits from the training for the company, ^ the increased productivity of the team.
3 The team's productivity has gone up by 10%, ^ the increased number of completed tasks in the past month.
4 Everyone's active listening skills have improved. Masha ^ has become a good listener since doing the program.
5 Sam and Pablo now work together more effectively. Sam makes a point of consulting Pablo about workflow issues, ^ prioritizing tasks on the schedule.
6 The team now deals with tasks in hand. ^ they focus more on getting things done and less on team politics.
7 The program has also resulted in an improvement in the way all team members deal with people outside the team, ^ their friendlier manner with support staff.

Transition words for highlighting and giving examples	
for instance	*specifically*
as demonstrated by	*as detailed in*
as shown by	*namely*
such as	*especially*
in particular	

b You are the social programming coordinator for a staff/student social club that is experiencing problems. Complete these sentences with your own ideas.

1 There has been little uptake of the program lately. For instance, …
2 Overall participation in the program in the past year has decreased, as detailed in …
3 Activities that involve … are especially …
4 Activities such as … are …

c Write sentences about the English language progress you and your classmates have made. Use transition words for highlighting and giving examples of particular achievements.

The ability of the class is improving, in particular our speaking skills.

d ⋙ Now go back to p. 89.

Neutral language	Persuasive language
in the city center	in the **heart** of the city
a different experience	a **unique** experience
high standards	**exacting** standards
well-trained	**highly** trained
make a dish	**create** a dish
We promise to …	Our **commitment** to you is …
our basic idea	our **core values**

Writing Tip

Many of the texts you read online are for promotion, and their aim is to persuade you to buy something, do something, or go somewhere. Notice how they use persuasive language, which makes things seem better, more positive, or more important.

a Choose the two words or phrases in *italics* in each sentence that work best as persuasive language.

1 Try one of our *freshly / lovingly / well-* prepared salads.
2 All our staff work to the *most exacting / highest / required* standards.
3 We *serve / offer / sell* light meals and snacks throughout the day.
4 Café Colombia is a *nice / perfect / ideal* place to meet your friends after work.
5 You can have *complete / some / total* confidence in our specialist products.
6 Why not spend a weekend *away from it all / in the countryside / far from the bustle of the city*?

b The sentences below promote different products and places. Which are for … ?

- a music venue
- a duty-free shop
- an airport lounge
- a bank
- a language school
- a furniture store
- a hotel

1 *With good furniture* and each with its own individual character, our rooms offer a *really quiet* atmosphere in which to unwind after a hard day's work.
2 Our beds are *of good quality* and will *be usable for many years*.
3 We have *a lot of* perfumes, and our brands are *known everywhere*.
4 The Basement is *a good place* for parties and live music events.
5 Our *well*-equipped classrooms and *good* teachers will ensure that your course is *different from the usual*.
6 *You're welcome* in our executive suite, where you can *spend* your time between flights in *comfortable* surroundings.
7 *We aim* to provide *a safe place* for your financial investments.

c Replace the words in *italics* in **b** 1–7 with the phrases in the box to make the sentences sound more positive.

> tastefully furnished   a unique learning experience
> manufactured to the highest standards
> an extensive range of   an ideal venue
> highly qualified   truly relaxing   our mission is
> globally recognized   a secure home   luxurious
> stand the test of time   a warm welcome awaits you
> fully   while away

d Choose a place in your town (a store, a shopping mall, a sports facility, a hotel, a school or college). Write two sentences to promote it. Try to describe it as positively as possible.

e 💬 Read your sentences aloud and listen to other students. What positive features are they promoting?

f ≫ Now go back to p. 101.

9D Linking: reason and result

Reason	Result
One key factor is ... / One of the (main) reasons is ... ... because of / due to ... ... as a (direct) result / consequence of ...	lead to / result in / cause / mean that ... As a (direct) result / consequence ... Consequently ... ... thus / thereby / hence / therefore ...

Writing Tip

There are small differences in use between *thus / therefore* and *thereby*:

The government raised taxes, **thereby/thus/~~therefore~~** raising a lot of money. = direct result of action

The government raised taxes. **Therefore,/ Thus,/ ~~Thereby,~~** starting a business is a bad idea. = logical conclusion

a Complete the sentences with the reason and result language in the box.

due to   resulted in   thus   cause
thereby   one of the main reasons

1 _____ people leave small towns is the lack of a lively cultural life.
2 Climate change has negatively affected rural environments and _____ urban migration.
3 At first, one or two family members move to the city and do well. _____ more family members join them, motivated by the hope to also do well.
4 There is sometimes disharmony in city neighborhoods _____ the pressure urban migration puts on infrastructure and amenities.
5 Dramatic population decreases can _____ the social fabric of rural communities to disappear altogether.
6 The exodus of inhabitants from small towns leads to less demand for goods and services, and _____ the closure of many businesses.

b Correct the reason and result language in these examples.

1 The recent arrival of large numbers of people from the countryside leads to the current shortage in housing.
2 Increased pressure on city infrastructure often causes that there is a rise in taxes.
3 There are fewer jobs in small towns because the closure of so many businesses.
4 As a result the arrival of immigrants, city schools have many more children enrolled.
5 Youth unemployment is very high in the town, thereby there's a lot of competition for jobs.

c Write four sentences about present or future changes in your neighborhood, using reason and result language.

In my neighborhood, a new sports center will be built due to the fundraising efforts of the local community. As a consequence, ...

d >>> Now go back to p. 113.

10D Movie reviews; Concise description

Ways to give information concisely	Examples
1 Add phrases between commas	Roy McBride, **a young astronaut**, goes in search of his father.
2 Add phrases before noun	**Young astronaut** Roy McBride goes in search of his father.
3 Use past participle clauses	Ad Astra, **directed by James Gray**, blends sci-fi with personal feeling.
4 Use present participle clauses	Roy McBride, **wanting to reach his father**, hijacks a spaceship.

a Use one or more of the ways shown in the chart to make these sentences more concise.

1 The first *Blade Runner* movie, which is directed by Ridley Scott, is a sci-fi classic.
2 When he realizes that his father is probably still alive, he decides he must reach him at all costs.
3 Alfonso Cuarón, who is a Mexican director, is planning to make a new movie.
4 Because she is determined to solve the crime, she works on the case night and day.
5 Jo March, who is the second oldest sister, is played by Saoirse Ronan.
6 Panem, which is a totalitarian country that is set in the future, is divided into 12 districts.

7 Because they are trapped in the mountains and because they know their food is running out, they send four people off to get help.

b Write about a movie you saw recently.

Write some basic information about it (name, director, outline of the story) in only three sentences.

Include at least two of the ways shown in the chart to make the information more concise.

c Read your sentences aloud, but don't say the name of the movie. Can other students guess the movie?

d Now think of a movie you did not enjoy. Replace the words in *italics* with your own ideas and continue each sentence concisely.

James Gray's latest movie, *Ad Astra,* is the *exciting and absorbing* story of ... .
A critical and box office hit, the movie has ...
Brad Pitt is perfectly cast in the role of ...
Tommy Lee Jones is also *superb* as ...
The movie provides a subtle portrayal of ...
The plot focuses on ...
It's an *original, thought-provoking* movie, and *certainly worth seeing*.

e >>> Now go back to p. 125.

Verb patterns

When followed by another verb (and object) (and indirect object), individual verbs follow different patterns:

verb + sb/sth + base form
She *makes me wash* the dishes.
I *saw the bus arrive*.

verb + infinitive
She *agreed to give* a presentation next week.
He *tends not to be* comfortable with new people.

verb + sb/sth + infinitive
I *asked the guests to wait* outside.
They *want him to come* to the party.

verb (+ sb/sth) + verb + -*ing*
He *admitted cheating* on the test.
He *hates us visiting* unannounced.

verb + preposition (+ sb/sth) + verb + -*ing*
I'm *concentrating on studying* this weekend.
She *insisted on him leaving* at three.

Some verbs have different meanings in different patterns.

admit	verb + verb + -*ing*
admit to	verb + preposition (+ sb/sth) + verb + -*ing*
advise	verb + sb/sth + infinitive verb + verb + -*ing*
agree	verb + infinitive
aim	verb + infinitive
allow	verb + sb/sth + infinitive verb + verb + -*ing*
anticipate	verb + verb + -*ing*
appear	verb + infinitive
appreciate	verb (+ sb/sth) + verb + -*ing*
approve of	verb + preposition (+ sb/sth) + verb + -*ing*
argue about	verb + preposition (+ sb/sth) + verb + -*ing*
arrange	verb + infinitive
ask	verb + (sb/sth) + infinitive
attempt	verb + infinitive
avoid	verb (+ sb/sth) + verb + -*ing*
beg	verb + (sb/sth) + infinitive
begin	verb + infinitive
believe in	verb + preposition + verb + -*ing*
can afford	verb + infinitive
can't help	verb + verb + -*ing*
can't stand	verb (+ sb/sth) + verb + -*ing*
care about	verb + preposition + sb/sth + verb + -*ing*
challenge	verb + sb/sth + infinitive
choose	verb + (sb/sth) + infinitive
claim	verb + infinitive
consider	verb + verb + -*ing*
continue	verb + infinitive verb + verb + -*ing*
*dare	verb + infinitive (be brave enough) verb + (sb/sth) + infinitive (challenge sb)
decide	verb + infinitive
demand	verb + infinitive
deny	verb + verb + -*ing*

demand	verb + infinitive
deserve	verb + infinitive
discuss	verb (+ sb/sth) + verb + -*ing*
dislike	verb (+ sb/sth) + verb + -*ing*
encourage	verb + sb/sth + infinitive
enjoy	verb (+ sb/sth) + verb + -*ing*
expect	verb (+ sb/sth) + infinitive
fail	verb + infinitive
feel (sense)	verb + sb/sth + base form
feel like	verb + preposition + verb + -*ing*
finish	verb + verb + -*ing*
*forget	verb + infinitive (an obligation) verb + verb + -*ing* (an event)
forget about	verb + preposition (+ sb/sth) + verb + -*ing*
forbid	verb + sb/sth + infinitive verb + verb + -*ing*
force	verb + sb/sth + infinitive
get (opportunity)	verb + infinitive
*go on	verb + infinitive (do a new activity) verb + verb + -*ing* (continue same activity)
happen	verb + infinitive
hate	verb (+ sb/sth) + infinitive verb (+ sb/sth) + verb + -*ing*
hear (noise)	verb + sb/sth + base form
help	verb (+ sb/sth) (+ *to*) + base form
hope	verb + infinitive
imagine	verb (+ sb/sth) + verb + -*ing*
insist on	verb + preposition (+ sb/sth) + verb + -*ing*
instruct	verb + sb/sth + infinitive
intend	verb (+ sb/sth) + infinitive
invite	verb + sb/sth + infinitive
involve	verb (+ sb/sth) + verb + -*ing*
keep	verb + verb + -*ing*
learn	verb + infinitive
let	verb + sb/sth + base form
like	verb (+ sb/sth) + infinitive verb (+ sb/sth) + verb + -*ing*
long	verb + infinitive
love	verb (+ sb/sth) + infinitive verb (+ sb/sth) + verb + -*ing*
make	verb + sb/sth + base form
manage	verb + infinitive
mention	verb (+ sb/sth) + verb + -*ing*
mind	verb (+ sb/sth) + verb + -*ing*
miss	verb (+ sb/sth) + verb + -*ing*
motivate	verb + sb/sth + infinitive
need	verb (+ sb/sth) + infinitive
notice	verb + sb/sth + base form
object to	verb + preposition (+ sb/sth) + verb + -*ing*
offer	verb + infinitive
order	verb + sb/sth + infinitive
pay	verb + sb/sth + infinitive
permit	verb + sb/sth + infinitive verb + verb + -*ing*

persuade	verb + sb/sth + infinitive
plan	verb + infinitive
plan on	verb + preposition + sb/sth + verb + -*ing*
postpone	verb + verb + -*ing*
practice	verb + verb + -*ing*
prefer	verb (+ sb/sth) + infinitive
prepare	verb (+ sb/sth) + infinitive
pretend	verb + infinitive
proceed	verb + infinitive
propose	verb + infinitive
recall	verb + verb + -*ing*
recommend	verb + verb + -*ing*
refuse	verb + infinitive
regret	verb + verb + -*ing*
*remember	verb + infinitive (an obligation) verb (+ sb/sth) + verb + -*ing* (an event)
remind	verb + sb/sth + infinitive
require	verb + sb/sth + infinitive
resent	verb (+ sb/sth) + verb + -*ing*
resist	verb (+ sb/sth) + verb + -*ing*
resume	verb + verb + -*ing*
risk	verb (+ sb/sth) + verb + -*ing*
say	verb + infinitive (instructions)
see	verb + sb/sth + base form
seem	verb + infinitive
start	verb + infinitive
*stop	verb (+ sb/sth) + infinitive (purpose of stopping) verb (+ sb/sth) + verb + -*ing* (activity)
succeed in	verb + preposition + verb + -*ing*
suggest	verb + sb + base form verb + verb + -*ing*
swear	verb + infinitive
talk about	verb + preposition (+ sb/sth) + verb + -*ing*
teach	verb + sb/sth + infinitive
tell	verb + sb/sth + infinitive (instruction)
tend	verb + infinitive
think about	verb + preposition (+ sb/sth) + verb + -*ing*
threaten	verb + infinitive
tolerate	verb (+ sb/sth) + verb + -*ing*
*try	verb + verb + -*ing* (a new activity) verb + infinitive (unsure of success)
understand	verb (+ sb/sth) + verb + -*ing*
urge	verb + sb/sth + infinitive
want	verb + sb/sth + infinitive
warn	verb + sb/sth + infinitive
watch	verb + sb/sth + base form
worry about	verb + preposition (+ sb/sth) + verb + -*ing*
would like / love / hate / prefer, etc.	verb (+ sb/sth) + infinitive

Phonemic symbols

Vowel sounds

/ə/	/æ/	/ʊ/	/ɑ/
teach**er**	m**a**n	p**u**t	g**o**t
/ɪ/	/i/	/e/	/ʌ/
ch**i**p	happ**y**	m**e**n	b**u**t

/ɜ/	/ɑ/	/u/	/ɔ/
sh**ir**t	p**ar**t	wh**o**	w**a**lk

Diphthongs (two vowel sounds)

/eə/	/ɪə/	/ɔɪ/	/aɪ/	/eɪ/	/oʊ/	/aʊ/
h**ai**r	n**ear**	b**oy**	f**i**ne	l**a**te	c**oa**t	n**ow**

Consonants

/p/	/b/	/f/	/v/	/t/	/d/	/k/	/g/	/θ/	/ð/	/tʃ/	/dʒ/
pill	**b**ook	**f**ace	**v**an	**t**ime	**d**og	**c**old	**g**o	**th**irty	**th**ey	**ch**oose	**j**eans
/s/	/z/	/ʃ/	/ʒ/	/m/	/n/	/ŋ/	/h/	/l/	/r/	/w/	/j/
say	**z**ero	**sh**op	u**s**ually	**m**e	**n**ow	si**ng**	**h**ot	**l**ate	**r**ed	**w**ent	**y**es

Irregular verbs

Infinitive	Past simple	Past participle
arise	arose	arisen
bear	bore	borne
beat	beat	beaten
bend	bent	bent
bet	bet	bet
bid	bid	bid
bind	bound	bound
blow	blew	blown
burn	burned/burnt	burned/burnt
burst	burst	burst
cling	clung	clung
deal	dealt	dealt
dwell	dwelt	dwelt
feed	fed	fed
flee	fled	fled
forbid	forbade	forbidden
foresee	foresaw	foreseen
hang	hung	hung
lay	laid	laid
lead	led	led
leap	leaped/leapt	leaped/leapt
lie	lay	lain
light	lit	lit
offset	offset	offset
overdo	overdid	overdone

Infinitive	Past simple	Past participle
overhear	overheard	overheard
overtake	overtook	overtaken
rebuild	rebuilt	rebuilt
rethink	rethought	rethought
rise	rose	risen
seek	sought	sought
set	set	set
shake	shook	shaken
shine	shined/shone	shined/shone
shoot	shot	shot
shrink	shrank	shrunk
shut	shut	shut
sink	sank	sunk
smell	smelled/smelt	smelled/smelt
sow	sowed	sown
spin	spun	spun
split	split	split
spread	spread	spread
swear	swore	sworn
sweep	swept	swept
swing	swung	swung
tear	tore	torn
undo	undid	undone
upset	upset	upset
wind	wound	wound

Acknowledgments

Author

The authors and publishers acknowledge the following sources of copyright material and are grateful for the permissions granted. While every effort has been made, it has not always been possible to identify the sources of all the material used, or to trace all copyright holders. If any omissions are brought to our notice, we will be happy to include the appropriate acknowledgements on reprinting and in the next update to the digital edition, as applicable.

Key:
U = Unit, C = Communication, V= Vocabulary, W= Writing.

Text

U7: Excerpt and Listening (Audio Script) from 'A lie detector on your phone' by Ian Goldin, *Future 60 second idea, BBC World Service*, 16/06/2014. Copyright 2014 © BBC Worldwide Limited. Reproduced with permission; Excerpt and Listening (Audio Script) from 'A remote that can reduce street noises' by Anja Kanngiese, *Future 60 second idea, BBC World Service*, 26/09/2013. Copyright 2013 © BBC Worldwide Limited. Reproduced with permission; Excerpt and Listening (Audio Script) from 'Job candidates must wear masks' by Maurice Fraser, *Future 60 second idea, BBC World Service*, 25/02/2012. Copyright 2012 © BBC Worldwide Limited. Reproduced with permission; Solo Syndication for the extract from 'Rise of the Machines: Meet Bina48, the robot who can tell jokes, recite poetry and mimic humans with startling ease' by Emily Anne Epstein, *Mail Online*, 19/07/2012. Copyright © 2012 MailOnline. All rights reserved. Distributed by Solo Syndication; Excerpt from 'Rewire: Digital Cosmopolitans in the Age of Connection' by Ethan Zuckerman. Copyright © Ethan Zuckerman. Reproduced with permission of WW.Norton & Company,Inc.; Guardian News & Media Ltd for the adapted text from 'This column will change your life: loneliness and temperature' by Oliver Burkeman, *The Guardian*, 01/06/2013. Copyright © 2014 Guardian News & Media Ltd. Reproduced with permission; **U8:** Excerpt and Listening (Audio Script) from 'Can extreme calorie counting make you live longer?' by Peter Bowes, *BBC World Service*, 24/03/2013. Copyright 2013 © BBC Worldwide Limited. Reproduced with permission; Excerpt from 'Segmented sleep: Ten strange things people do at night' and 'The myth of the eight-hour sleep', by Stephanie Hegarty, *BBC News Magazine*, 22/02/2012. Copyright 2012 © BBC Worldwide Limited. Reproduced with kind permission; Guardian News & Media Ltd for the adapted text from 'Aubrey de Grey: We don't have to get sick as we get older' by Caspar Llewellyn Smith, *The Guardian*, 01/08/2010. Copyright © 2010 Guardian News & Media Ltd. Reproduced with permission; **U9:** Text about Jeanne Gang. Reproduced with kind permission of Studio Gang; **U10:** Text about Scott Berkun. Reproduced with kind permission of Scott Berkun.

Photographs

The following photographs are sourced from Getty Images.

U6: Getty Images/Handout/Getty Images Entertainment; Mireya Acierto/Getty Images Entertainment; Igor Ustynskyy/Moment; Jesus Trillo Lago/iStock/Getty Images Plus; Westend61; Plume Creative/DigitalVision; Simonkr/E+; Runstudio/Moment; Fizkes/iStock/Getty Images Plus; Manuel Sulzer/Cultura; Grandriver/E+; SolStock/E+; **U7:** BSIP/Universal Images Group; VCG/Visual China Group; Fort Worth Star-Telegram/Tribune News Service; Jacobs Stock Photography Ltd/DigitalVision; Jose Luis Pelaez Inc/DigitalVision; Westend61; Roydee/E+; Eclipse_images/E+; MarianVejcik/iStock/Getty Images Plus; Creative-Family/iStock/Getty Images Plus; Maskot/DigitalVision; Mohamad Itani/Photodisc; Hinterhaus Productions/DigitalVision; Andresr/E+; Muntz/The Image Bank/Getty Images Plus; Sturti/E+; ColorBlind Images/The Image Bank/Getty Images Plus; Philipp Nemenz/DigitalVision; Jupiterimages/Photos.com/Getty Images Plus; Klaus Tiedge; **U8:** Laflor/E+; Tara Moore/Stone; Skaman306/Moment; Monkeybusinessimages/iStock/Getty Images Plus; JohnnyGreig/iStock/Getty Images Plus; Westend61; Ajr_images/iStock/Getty Images Plus; BSIP/UIG; Motortion/iStock/Getty Images Plus; Cuiphoto/iStock/Getty Images Plus; GlobalP/iStock/Getty Images Plus; DanielPrudek/iStock/Getty Images Plus; GMint/iStock/Getty Images Plus; Evgeniy1/iStock/Getty Images Plus; Hindustan Times; Malikov Aleksandr/iStock/Getty Images Plus; SergeyChayko/iStock/Getty Images Plus; Fascinadora/iStock/Getty Images Plus; Supamas Ihakjit/iStock/Getty Images Plus; JohnArcher/iStock/Getty Images Plus; Alvarez/E+; By_nicholas/E+; Simonlong/Moment; Jasmin Merdan/Moment; Burcu Atalay Tankut/Moment; Karamba70/iStock/Getty Images Plus; Thomas Barwick/Photodisc; **U9:** VCG/Visual China Group; Calin Hertioga/Moment; Markpittimages/iStock Editorial/Getty Images Plus; Alastair James/iStock Editorial/Getty Images Plus; Jeff Greenberg/Universal Images Group; Education Images/Universal Images Group; Portland Press

Herald; VvoeVale/iStock Editorial/Getty Images Plus; Katatonia82/iStock Editorial/Getty Images Plus; Lukasz Wisniewski/EyeEm; NurPhoto; Domingo Leiva/Moment; S. Greg Panosian/E+; Chicago Tribune/Tribune News Service; Raymond Boyd/Michael Ochs Archives; Interim Archives/Archive Photos; Gary Hershorn/Corbis News; Photofusion/Universal Images Group; Funky-data/E+; Skynesher/E+; David Clapp/Stone; Mark Meredith/Moment; iShootPhotosLLC/iStock; Chameleonseye/iStock/Getty Images Plus; Mihailomilovanovic/E+; **U10:** Jason Connolly/AFP; E. Neitzel/WireImage; Paul Bruinooge/Patrick McMullan; Isa Foltin/WireImage; Alberto E. Rodriguez/Getty Images Entertainment; Ned Frisk; Klaus Vedfelt/DigitalVision; SDI Productions/E+; Cmannphoto/E+; Klikk/iStock/Getty Images Plus; Filipefrazao/iStock/Getty Images Plus; YinYang/iStock/Getty Images Plus; Pablo Porciuncula Brune/AFP; Simon Stacpoole/Offside; Gallo Images/Getty Images Sport; Julian Finney/Getty Images Sport; Mediaphotos/E+; PeopleImages/E+; Boston Globe; Rick Partington/EyeEm; Cokada/E+; **C:** Teeramet Thanomkiat/EyeEm; Dean Mitchell/E+; Bertram Henry/Stone/Getty Images Plus; Westend61; PhotoAlto/Frederic Cirou/PhotoAlto Agency RF Collections; AndreyPopov/iStock/Getty Images Plus; Njekaterina/The Image Bank/Getty Images Plus; Yuin Lu Hoo/E+; Alison Taylor Photograpy/iStock/Getty Images Plus; Dennis Walton/Lonely Planet Images/Getty Images Plus; Wootthisak nirongboot/Moment; JGI/Jamie Grill; Lars Ruecker/Moment/Getty Images Plus; Henrik Sorensen/DigitalVision; **V:** Mediaphotos/E+; Jasmin Merdan/Moment; Fuse/Corbis; Thierry Grun/Photolibrary/Getty Images Plus; Scott Markewitz; Mike Powell/Taxi/Getty Images Plus; Blackred/E+; Lydelter Bolodin/EyeEm; Glowimages; Hisham Ibrahim/Photographer's Choice/Getty Images Plus; Zero Creatives/Cultura; RubberBall Productions/Brand X Pictures; Alexa Miller/The Image Bank/Getty Images Plus; Witthaya Prasongsin/Moment; FlairImages/iStock/Getty Images Plus; Bolot/E+; Richard Boll/Photolibrary/Getty Images Plus; Richard Fearon/EyeEm; Westend61; Roger Tidman/Corbis Documentary; Franckreporter/iStock/Getty Images Plus; IAISI/Moment; Tuomas Lehtinen/Moment; Viktoryia Vinnikava/EyeEm; Mark Newman/The Image Bank; LordRunar/E+; Eddie Brady/The Image Bank; Joseph Gardner/Moment; Bulgac/E+; Chiara Cattaruzzi Photography/Moment; Grant Faint/The Image Bank; Aitor Diago/Moment; XiXinXing; Adamkaz/E+; Mariana Alija/Moment; Steve Dunwell/Photographer's Choice/Getty Images Plus; Hal Bergman/Stone; Blueflames/iStock/Getty Images Plus; Boyshots/iStock/Getty Images Plus; Marje/E+; Tom Sibley/The Image Bank; Franck-Boston/iStock/Getty Images Plus; Danita Delimont/Gallo Images/Getty Images Plus; Jenny Jones/Lonely Planet Images/Getty Images Plus; Stevens Frémont/The Image Bank; Prostock-Studio/iStock/Getty Images Plus; Morsa Images/E+; Comstock/Stockbyte; Mayur Kakade/Moment; Alberto Cassani/Moment; Burazin/The Image Bank/Getty Images Plus; **W:** ElOjoTorpe/Moment; Kelly Cheng/Moment; M_a_y_a/iStock/Getty Images Plus; Eak8dda/iStock/Getty Images Plus; Koron/Moment; Zolga_F/iStock/Getty Images Plus; Khaichuin Sim/Moment; Shalom Ormsby Images Inc/DigitalVision.

The following photographs are sourced from other libraries/sources. **U6:** © Elliott Erwitt/Magnum Photos; **U7:** Dpa Picture Alliance/Alamy Stock Photo; **U9:** © Museo Soumaya.Fundación Carlos Slim; **U10:** Copyright © Scott Berkun.

Cover photography by Stephen Frink/The Image Bank/Getty Images.

Illustrations

David Semple; Gavin Reece (New Division); Jérôme Mireault (Colagene); Marie-Eve Tremblay (Colagene); Mark Bird; Martin Sanders (Beehive); QBS Learning; Phil Hackett; Roger Penwill; Rosie Scott (NB Illustration).

Audio produced by John Marshall Media.

Corpus

Development of this publication has made use of the Cambridge English Corpus (CEC). The CEC is a computer database of contemporary spoken and written English, which currently stands at over one billion words. It includes British English, American English and other varieties of English. It also includes the Cambridge Learner Corpus, developed in collaboration with the University of Cambridge

ESOL Examinations. Cambridge University Press has built up the CEC to provide evidence about language use that helps us to produce better language teaching materials.

English Profile
This product is informed by English Vocabulary Profile, built as part of English Profile, a collaborative program designed to enhance the learning, teaching and assessment of English worldwide. Its main funding partners are Cambridge University Press and Cambridge Assessment English and its aim is to create a "profile" for English, linked to the Common European Framework of Reference for Languages (CEFR). English Profile outcomes, such as the English Vocabulary Profile, will provide detailed information about the language that learners can be expected to demonstrate at each CEFR level, offering a clear benchmark for learners' proficiency. For more information, please visit www.englishprofile.org.

CALD
The Cambridge Advanced Learner's Dictionary is the world's most widely used dictionary for learners of English. Including all the words and phrases that learners are likely to come across, it also has easy-to-understand definitions and example sentences to show how the word is used in context. The Cambridge Advanced Learner's Dictionary is available online at dictionary.cambridge.org.

CAMBRIDGE
UNIVERSITY PRESS

University Printing House, Cambridge CB2 8BS, United Kingdom

One Liberty Plaza, 20th Floor, New York, NY 10006, USA

477 Williamstown Road, Port Melbourne, VIC 3207, Australia

314–321, 3rd Floor, Plot 3, Splendor Forum, Jasola District Centre, New Delhi – 110025, India

103 Penang Road, #05–06/07, Visioncrest Commercial, Singapore 238467

Cambridge University Press is part of the University of Cambridge.

It furthers the University's mission by disseminating knowledge in the pursuit of education, learning and research at the highest international levels of excellence.

www.cambridge.org
Information on this title: www.cambridge.org/9781108861519

© Cambridge University Press 2022

First published 2022

20 19 18 17 16 15 14 13 12 11 10 9 8 7 6 5 4 3 2 1

Printed in Great Britain by CPI Group (UK) Ltd, Croydon CR0 4YY

A catalogue record for this publication is available from the British Library

ISBN 978-1-108-81721-9 Advanced Student's Book with eBook
ISBN 978-1-108-79801-3 Advanced Student's Book A with eBook
ISBN 978-1-108-79802-0 Advanced Student's Book B with eBook
ISBN 978-1-108-86144-1 Advanced Student's Book with Digital Pack
ISBN 978-1-108-86150-2 Advanced Student's Book A with Digital Pack
ISBN 978-1-108-86151-9 Advanced Student's Book B with Digital Pack
ISBN 978-1-108-81735-6 Advanced Workbook with Answers
ISBN 978-1-108-81736-3 Advanced Workbook A with Answers
ISBN 978-1-108-81737-0 Advanced Workbook B with Answers
ISBN 978-1-108-81738-7 Advanced Workbook without Answers
ISBN 978-1-108-81739-4 Advanced Workbook A without Answers
ISBN 978-1-108-81740-0 Advanced Workbook B without Answers
ISBN 978-1-108-81741-7 Advanced Full Contact with eBook
ISBN 978-1-108-81742-4 Advanced Full Contact A with eBook
ISBN 978-1-108-81744-8 Advanced Full Contact B with eBook
ISBN 978-1-108-86147-2 Advanced Full Contact with Digital Pack
ISBN 978-1-108-86148-9 Advanced Full Contact A with Digital Pack
ISBN 978-1-108-86149-6 Advanced Full Contact B with Digital Pack
ISBN 978-1-108-79803-7 Advanced Teacher's Book with Digital Pack
ISBN 978-1-108-79808-2 Advanced Presentation Plus

Additional resources for this publication at www.cambridge.org/americanempower

This page is intentionally left blank.

This page is intentionally left blank.